KV-310-055

KNOWLEDGE MANAGEMENT:

The Bibliography

Compiled by

Paul R. Burden

**American Society for
Information Science
and Technology**

ASIST Monograph Series

Ⅲ **Information Today, Inc.**
Medford, New Jersey

Original version created by Morgen MacIntosh and T. Kanti Srikantaiah and published
in *Knowledge Management for the Information Professional*.

First printing, October 2000

Knowledge Management: The Bibliography

Copyright © 2000 by American Society for Information Science and Technology

All rights reserved. No part of this book may be reproduced in any form or by any electronic or mechanical means including information storage and retrieval systems without permission in writing from the publisher, except by a reviewer, who may quote brief passages in a review. Published by Information Today, Inc., 143 Old Marlton Pike, Medford, New Jersey 08055.

Prepared under the editorial supervision of Prof. T. Kanti Srikantaiah, Ph. D., Director, Center for Knowledge Management, Dominican University, River Forest, IL. Concept designed by T. Kanti Srikantaiah. Original version created by Morgen MacIntosh and T. Kanti Srikantaiah and published in *Knowledge Management for the Information Professional.*

Printed and bound in the United States of America.

Library of Congress Cataloging-in-Publication Data

Burden, Paul R.
    Knowledge management : the bibliography / Paul Burden.
      p. cm.
    [Based on the bibliography originally] "Created by Morgen MacIntosh and T. Kanti Srikantaiah and published in Knowledge management for the information professional." "This bibliography is being used by the Center for Knowledge Management at Dominican University as an adjunct to course syllabi and textbooks ... and was also used in and evaluated at the KM 2000 Workshop held on November 12, 1999 and March 17, 2000 ... sponsored by the Center"—P. B.
    Includes index.
    ISBN 1-57387-101-X
    1. Knowledge management—Bibliography. I. MacIntosh, Morgen. II. Srikantaiah, T. Kanti III. KM 2000 Workshop (1999 and 2000 : Dominican University, River Forest, Ill.) IV. Knowledge management for the information professional. V. Title.

    Z7164.07 B847 2000
    [HD30.2]
    016.6584'038—dc21

                                       00-56698

Publisher: Thomas H. Hogan, Sr.
Editor-in-Chief: John B. Bryans
Managing Editor: Janet M. Spavlik
Production Manager: M. Heide Dengler
Cover Designer: Jacqueline Walter
Book Designer: Jeremy M. Pellegrin
Indexer: Sharon Hughes

Rotherham Health Care Library

HP01636

WITHDRAWN FROM
ROTHERHAM RFT LIBRARY
& KNOWLEDGE SERVICE

**Tools for Health Library
& Knowledge Services**

Return to:
Interlibrary Loans
Health Care Library
District General Hospital
Rotherham
S60 2UD

*Funded by a grant from the
Trent NHS Knowledge &
Library Services Unit*

13.99
0%
spec
app

-DEDICATION-

This work is dedicated to Frances
for her constant and absolute support.

TABLE OF CONTENTS

NUMBER OF CITATIONS

ACKNOWLEDGMENTS

I would like to acknowledge the contributions of the following individuals:

T. Kanti Srikantaiah, Ph.D.: Dr. Srikantaiah originally offered me this project, and then encouraged me to take it to another level. I am grateful for his monumental assistance, commentary, encouragement, and support in this undertaking.

Morgen MacIntosh: I should like to acknowledge her generosity as well as her hard work and quality effort. The foundation upon which I have built was a tough act to follow. I hope my additions have complemented her extraordinary efforts.

Michael Koenig, Ph.D.: Dr. Koenig introduced me to the field of Knowledge Management and emphasized the importance and value of publishing, regardless of one's field of endeavor.

Catherine Mattson: Her "new eyes" helped ensure that this work is consistent. It is better after her assistance because her criticisms and suggestions were useful as well as valid.

I should also like to acknowledge the contributions of my other colleagues who directly or indirectly recommended quality sources that found their way into this book.

INTRODUCTION

Knowledge Management has taken the business world by storm—and rightfully so. The concepts espoused in Knowledge Management are not only logical, they have also been proven to work in the most competitive environment imaginable—real life. Knowledge Management is more than a company executive writing a memo, the company purchasing groupware, managing a collection of explicit materials, applying a fragmented policy, and creating an intranet. Having this narrow perception of Knowledge Management is akin to blind men describing an elephant by touch. Each will be correct in the perception of a part of the elephant, but they will not grasp the concept of the whole.

Knowledge Management is not a procedure or a policy. Knowledge Management is a holistic process that demands a total organizational commitment to cooperation in order to succeed. It is a process that has a beginning—an evolutionary process with products—but has no end if pursued properly. As an organization evolves, Knowledge Management must evolve right along with it. John Browne of BP has referred to the "shrinking half-life of ideas"; a good, even great idea will not keep an organization afloat indefinitely. Changes in the market, changes in the competition, and even changes within the company itself force the firm to remain abreast of the most recent developments in its situation. How does it discover and react to these changes? Information. If a company cannot access, store, retrieve, and provide the information to the proper individuals in a timely manner, then the firm will eventually fail. Knowledge Management gives the organization the opportunity to fully utilize *all* of its assets. This Bibliography is an attempt to collect some of the literature in a useful format for the individual interested in Knowledge Management.

Professionals who are active in the field are probably familiar with most, if not all, of the authors and material cited here. Hopefully, there will be something new that will assist the user, regardless of his/her skill or knowledge level. Who, then, is the intended audience for this work?

Active Knowledge Professionals can use this as a reference tool to seek new information or to locate previously missed materials.

New members of the profession can use it as a starting point: a guide to allow them to see some of the literature that is available in the various subject areas of Knowledge Management.

Knowledge Management students can use it as a suggested reading list: a reference tool to determine if the field offers a specific subject area within the scope of their interests or expertise.

Anyone who wants to get an idea of what is being discussed and pursued in this interesting new field can use it as well.

This Bibliography is being used by the Center for Knowledge Management at Dominican University as an adjunct to course syllabi and textbooks. It has been examined at length by students in the Knowledge

Management courses offered, and I appreciate and have incorporated some the comments and suggestions that have been made.

The Bibliography was also used in and evaluated at the KM 2000 Workshop held on November 12, 1999 and March 17, 2000. This event was sponsored by the Center for Knowledge Management at Dominican University in River Forest, IL. The participants at this seminar are active in various disciplines throughout the United States.

Methodology

The methodology used to compile this bibliography is as follows:

- Books: review of available books at Books in Print, WorldCat, amazon.com, and barnesandnoble.com using "Intellectual Capital" and "Knowledge Management" as keywords in the searches. Abstracts, the books themselves, or reviews have been used to determine the inclusion of a document.

- Articles: Boolean search of thirty-four databases using "Intellectual Capital" and "Knowledge Management" plus the various subheadings as keywords, and review of abstracts or reviews.

- Videos: review of available videos at amazon.com, and barnesand noble.com using "Intellectual Capital" and "Knowledge Management" as keywords in the searches.

- Web Sites: Boolean search of the Internet itself and NetFirst using "Intellectual Capital" and "Knowledge Management" as keywords.

Bibliography Formats

There is a brief introduction and description of the materials included in each of the sections of the Bibliography. In the Article Section, not only does it have an introduction, each subheading in the Article Section also has a brief introduction and description of the materials contained within. The citations follow.

Citation Formats

Books: Author(s), Compiler(s), and Editor(s). *Title*. Place of publication: Publisher, Date of Publication.

Articles: Author(s), Compiler(s), Editor(s). "Article Title." *Publication Title* Volume.Number (Date): Pagination.

Web Sites: (Viewed between January and July 2000)
Institution Name or Web Site Title. Web Address.

Videos: Title. Place of Publication: Publisher, Date of Publication.

When compiling a bibliography, the word "comprehensive" makes one nervous, especially in a field that is growing as rapidly as Knowledge Management. Articles, books, lectures, videos, and web sites are being published and put online as fast as they can be created. At the present time, there are thousands of articles and hundreds of books devoted to the field of Knowledge Management. Obviously, a line must be drawn in order to publish the Bibliography. The compilation could conceivably go on and on...

I think one would be very hard-pressed to keep current with the literature in Knowledge Management due to the explosive growth of the field. The continuing growth of the field indicates that Knowledge Management is not, as some have said, a flash in the pan. If Knowledge Management was a flash in the pan, then not only would the volume of literature decrease, Knowledge Management would not enjoy the growth that it does on a global scale. Knowledge Management has also shown the flexibility to be applied in virtually every knowledge-related field from academia to business strategy, and decision-making to the sciences—both physical and social.

This is not the only attempt to collect and categorize the literature of Knowledge Management on this level, just the first.

Paul R. Burden
Librarian
DeVry Institute of Technology
Tinley Park, IL

Note: The citations are as complete as the source would allow.

BOOKS

The literature of Knowledge Management, as in most disciplines, began with the publication of articles in professional journals and the presentation of papers at conferences. As the volume of available information increased, the next logical step in the accumulation, creation, and dissemination of a knowledge base was the production of books.

This list contains books published with "Intellectual Capital" or "Knowledge Management" as their primary focus as taken from Books in Print, WorldCat, and the inventories of amazon.com and barnesand noble.com. The two retail sources were selected because of the sheer volume of their respective inventories and sales. The books listed should be among the most current and most often-selected works available.

The bibliography includes books covering a wide variety of categories in both the Intellectual Capital and Knowledge Management subject areas. This bibliography includes books dealing with the beginnings of Knowledge Management: Peter M. Senge's *The Fifth Discipline: The Art and Practice of the Learning Organization*; KM and the art of management: Steven Albert and Keith Bradley's *Managing Knowledge: Experts, Agencies and Organizations*; the impact of KM abroad: the American Productivity and Quality Center's *Knowledge Management and the Learning Organization: A European Perspective*; KM and business strategy: J. Friso Den Hertog and Edward Huizenga's *The Knowledge Enterprise: Implementation of Intelligent Business Strategies*; and the impact of KM on continuing business practices: Dorothy Leonard-Barton's *Wellsprings of Knowledge: Building and Sustaining the Sources of Innovation*; and KM and its value to interdisciplinary studies: Kanti Srikantaiah and Michael Koenig's *Knowledge Management for the Information Professional*. One of the more recent books, Richard I. Henderson's *Compensation Management in a Knowledge-Based World*, covers a subject near and dear to everyone's heart.

The literature of Knowledge Management is growing day after day—a testament to the validity of the discipline. The list of books that follows, it is hoped, will give the reader not only an overall view of the Intellectual Capital and Knowledge Management literature that is available, but also will introduce some works devoted to specific areas of interest. The reader will find many familiar names here as well as the names of some new contributors to the field.

The books included here are not grouped under the subheadings used for the articles, but they are listed alphabetically by the surname of the author or editor.

Abdelguerfi, Mahdi and Simon Lavington, eds. *Emerging Trends in Database and Knowledge-Base Machines: The Application of Parallel Architectures to Smart Information Systems*. New York: Institute of Electrical & Electronic Engineering, 1995.

Abell, Angela. *Competing with Knowledge: The Information Professional in the Knowledge Management Age*. London: Library Association, 1999.

Abrams, Janet. *If/Then: Play*. Amsterdam: The Netherlands Institute, 1999.

Addleson, M. *Equilibrium Versus Understanding: Towards the Restoration of Economics as Social Theory*. New York: Routledge, 1995.

AGI Conference at GIS 98. Profiting from Collaboration. London: Association for Geographic Information & Miller Freeman UK Ltd, 1998.

Alavi, Maryam. *KPMG Peat Marwick US: One Giant Brain*. Boston: Harvard Business School Publishing, 1997.

Albert, Steven and Keith Bradley. *Managing Knowledge: Experts, Agencies and Organizations*. Cambridge, NY: Cambridge University Press, 1997.

Albrow, Martin. *Do Organizations Have Feelings?* New York: Routledge, 1997.

Alexander, James C. and Michael C. Lyons. *The Knowledge-Based Organization: Four Steps to Increasing Sales, Profits, and Market Share*. Burr Ridge, IL: Irwin Professional Publishing, 1994.

Allee, Verna. *The Knowledge Evolution: Expanding Organizational Intelligence*. Woburn, MA: Butterworth-Heinemann, 1997.

Alvarez, Jose Luis, ed. *The Diffusion and Consumption of Business Knowledge*. New York: St. Martin's Press, 1997.

Alvesson, Mats. *Management of Knowledge-Intensive Companies: De Gruyter Studies in Organization, 61*. Berlin: de Gruyter, 1995.

American Productivity and Quality Center. *Knowledge Management*. Houston, TX: American Productivity and Quality Center, 1996.

American Productivity and Quality Center. *Knowledge Management and the Learning Organization: A European Perspective*. Houston, TX: American Productivity and Quality Center, 1996.

American Productivity and Quality Center. *Knowledge Management Consortium Benchmarking Study: Best Practice Report*. Houston, TX: American Productivity and Quality Center, 1996.

American Productivity and Quality Center. *Managing Competitive Intelligence in a Global Economy*. Houston, TX: American Productivity and Quality Center, 1998.

American Productivity and Quality Center. *Using Information Technology to Support Knowledge Management, Consortium Benchmarking Study: Best Practice Report*. Houston, TX: American Productivity and Quality Center, 1997.

Amidon, Debra M. *Innovation Strategy for the Knowledge Economy: The Ken Awakening.* Woburn, MA: Butterworth-Heinemann, 1997.

Andersson, Oake E. et al. *Knowledge and Industrial Organization.* Berlin: Springer-Verlag, 1989.

Anger, Frank D., ed. *Industrial & Engineering Applications of Artificial Intelligence and Expert Systems.* Newark, NJ: Gordon and Breach, 1994.

Applehans, Wayne. *Managing Knowledge: A Practical Guide to Intranet-Based Knowledge Management.* Reading, MA: Addison Wesley Publishing Co., 1999.

Applehans, Wayne et al. *Managing Knowledge: A Practical Web-Based Approach.* Reading, MA: Addison Wesley Publishing Co., 1998.

Arbnor, Ingeman and Bjorn Bjerke. *Methodology for Creating Businesss Knowledge.* London: Sage Publications, 1996.

Argote, Linda. *Organizational Learning: Creating, Retaining, and Transferring Knowledge.* Boston: Kluwer Academic Publishing, 1999.

Argote, Linda. *The Psychological Foundations of Knowledge Transfer in Organizations.* San Diego, CA: Academic Press, 2000.

Argyris, C. and D. Schon. *Organizational Learning: A Theory of Action Perspective.* Reading, MA: Addison Wesley Publishing Co., 1978.

Argyris, Chris. *Knowledge for Action: A Guide to Overcoming Barriers to Organizational Change.* San Francisco: Jossey-Bass Publishers, 1993.

Armistead, Colin. *Knowledge Management.* London: Cassell Academic, 1999.

Arthur Andersen. *World Bank Knowledge Management Concept Paper: A Practical Approach.* Chicago: Arthur Andersen Business Consulting, 1996.

Badaracco, Joseph L., Jr. *The Knowledge Link: How Firms Compete Through Strategic Alliances.* Boston: Harvard Business School Press, 1991.

Baets, Walter R. J. *Organization Learning and Knowledge Technologies in a Dynamic Environment.* Boston: Kluwer Academic Publishing, 1998.

Bata, T., ed. *Knowledge in Action: The Bata System of Management.* Washington, DC: IOS Press, 1997.

Beaumont, John R. and Ewan Sutherland. *Information Resources Management: Management in Our Knowledge-Based Society and Economy.* Visby, Sweden: Books on Demand, 1992.

Bigelow, John D., ed. *Managerial Skills: Explorations in Practical Knowledge.* London: Sage Publications, 1991.

Bigus, Joseph P. *Data Mining with Neural Networks: Solving Business Problems from Application Development to Decision Support*. New York: McGraw-Hill Text, 1996.

Blair, J. *Key Issues for Knowledge Management*. Stamford, CT: Gartner Group Research Note/Key Issues K-KMGT-1650, 1997.

Boisot, Max H. *Knowledge Assets: Securing Competitive Advantage in the Information Economy*. New York: Oxford University Press, 1998.

Bontis, Nick. *Managing Knowledge by Diagnosing Organizational Learning Flows and Intellectual Capital Stocks: Framing and Advancing the Literature*. London: Richard Ivey School of Business University of Western Ontario, 1997.

Borghoff, Uwe and Remo Pareschi, eds. *Information Technology for Knowledge Management*. Berlin: Springer-Verlag, 1998.

Botkin, James W. *Smart Business: How Knowledge Communities Can Revolutionize Your Company*. New York: Free Press, 1999.

Breslin, Jud. *The Business Knowledge Repository*. Westport, CT: Greenwood Publishing Group, 1998.

Brooking, Annie. *Corporate Memory: Strategies for Knowledge Management*. London: International Thomson Business Press, 1999.

Brooking, Annie. *Dream Ticket: Corporate Strategy with Intellectual Capital*. London: International Thomson Business Press, 1999.

Brooking, Annie. *Intellectual Capital*. London: International Thomson Business Press, 1997.

Brooking, Annie. *Intellectual Capital: Core Assets for the Third Millenium*. London: International Thomson Business Press, 1996.

Brooks, L. and C. Kimble, eds. *Information Systems-The Next Generation. Proceedings of the 4th UKAIS Conference*. Maidenhead, UK: McGraw-Hill Publishing, 1999.

Brown, John Seely and Paul Duguid. *The Social Life of Information*. Boston: Harvard Business School Press, 2000.

Brush, Candida G. *Women-Owned Businesses: The State of Our Knowledge and Issues for the Future*. Boston: Boston University School of Management, 1995.

Buckholtz, Thomas J. *Information Proficiency: Your Key to the Information Age*. New York: John Wiley & Sons, 1997.

Bud-Frierman, Lisa, ed. *Information Acumen: The Understanding and Use of Knowledge in Modern Business*. New York: Routledge, 1994.

Bukowitz, Wendi and Ruth L. Williams. *Knowledge Management Fieldbook*. Lanham, MD: National Book Network, 1999.

Burton-Jones, Alan. *Knowledge Capitalism: Business, Work, and Learning in the New Economy.* Oxford: Oxford University Press, 1999.

Burwell, Helen et al. *Online Competitive Intelligence: Increase Your Profits Using Cyber Intelligence.* Tempe, AZ: Facts on Demand Press, 1999.

Butler, Janet G. *Information Technology: Converging Strategies and Trends for the 21st Century.* Portland, OR: Computer Research Technology Corp., 1997.

Buzan, Tony et al. *The Brainsmart Leader.* Brookfield, VT: Gower Publishing Co., 1999.

Caffrey, Larry. *Information Sharing Between and within Governments.* London: Commonwealth Secretariat, 1999.

Carlin, Stephanie et al. *Expanding Knowledge Management Externally: Putting Your Knowledge to Work for Customers.* Houston, TX: American Productivity and Quality Center, 1998.

Carter, Barry C. *Infinite Wealth: A New World of Collaboration and Abundance in the Knowledge Area.* Woburn, MA: Butterworth-Heinemann, 1999.

Chard, Ann Maria. *Knowledge Management at Ernst & Young.* Palo Alto, CA: Graduate School of Business Stanford University, 1997.

Chauvel, Daniel and Charles Despres. *Future Vision in Knowledge Management.* Oxford: Butterworth-Heinemann, 2000.

Chertavian, G. *Knowledge: Intellectual Capital and the Value Chain.* London: Uxbridge, 1998.

Choo, C. W. *The Knowing Organization: How Organizations Use Information to Construct Meaning, Create Knowledge, and Make Decisions.* New York: Oxford University Press, 1998.

Cios, Krzysztof J. et al. *Data Mining Methods for Knowledge Discovery.* Boston: Kluwer Academic Publishing, 1998.

Clare, Mark and Arthur W. DeTore. *Knowledge Assets: Professional's Guide to Valuation and Financial Management.* San Diego: Harcourt Professional Publishing, 2000.

Clark, K. et al., eds. *The Uneasy Alliance.* Boston: Harvard Business School Press, 1985.

Clark, Peter A. *Organisations in Action: Competition between Contexts.* New York: Routledge, 1999.

Clarke, Thomas. *Changing Paradigms: The Transformation of Management Knowledge for the 21st Century.* London: HarperCollinsBusiness, 1998.

Clegg, Stewart R. and Gill Palmer, eds. *The Politics of Knowledge Management: A Critical Perspective.* London: Sage Publications, 1996.

Cohen, Don. *Managing Knowledge for Business Success: Document 1194-97-CH*. New York: Conference Board, 1997.

Conceicao, Pedro et al., eds. *Science, Technology, and Innovation Policy: Opportunities and Challenges for the Knowledge Economy*. Westport, CT: Greenwood Publishing Group, 2000.

Cope, Mick. *Leading the Organisation to Learn: The 10 Levers for Putting Knowledge and Learning to Work*. London: Financial Times, 1998.

Cortada, James W. and John A. Woods, eds. *The 1998 ASTD Training and Performance Yearbook*. New York: McGraw-Hill, 1998.

Cortada, James W. and John A. Woods, eds. *Knowledge Management Yearbook 1999-2000*. Woburn, MA: Butterworth-Heinemann, 1999.

Cortada, James W. and John A. Woods, eds. *The Quality Yearbook: 1998 Edition*. New York: McGraw-Hill, 1998.

Cortada, James W. *Publishing Intellectual Capital: Getting Your Business into Print*. Upper Saddle River, NJ: Prentice Hall PTR, 1999.

Cortada, James W. *Rise of the Knowledge Worker*. Woburn, MA: Butterworth-Heinemann, 1998.

Cross, Robert L. *Strategic Learning in a Knowledge Economy: Individual, Collective and Organizational Learning Processes*. Woburn, MA: Butterworth-Heinemann, 1999.

Croy, Norvin et al. *Using Information Technology to Support Knowledge Management*. Houston, TX: American Productivity and Quality Center, 1997.

Cutcher-Gershenfeld, Joel et al. *Knowledge-Driven Work: Unexpected Lessons from Japanese and United States Work Practices*. Oxford: Oxford University Press, Lexington, KY: [S.N.], 1998.

Czarniawska, B. *Narrating the Organization: Dramas of Institutional Identity*. Chicago: University of Chicago Press, 1997.

Czerniawska, Fiona. *Management Consultancy in the 21st Century*. Lafayette, IN: Purdue University Press, 1999.

Data Warehousing & Data Mining: Implementing Strategic Knowledge Management. Portland, OR: Computer Research Technology Corporation, 1999.

Davè, Kshiti P. *An Investigation of Knowledge Management Characteristics: Synthesis, Delphi Study, Analysis*. Lexington, KY: [S.N.], 1998.

Davenport, Thomas H. and Laurence Prusak. *Information Ecology: Mastering the Information and Knowledge Environment*. New York: Oxford University Press, 1997.

Davenport, Thomas H. and Laurence Prusak. *Working Knowledge: How Organizations Manage What They Know.* Woburn, MA: Harvard Business School Press, 1998.

Dawson, Ross. *Developing Knowledge-Based Client Relationships: The Future of Professional Services.* Boston: Butterworth-Heinemann, 2000.

De Geus, Arie. *The Living Company.* Boston: Harvard Business School Press, 1997.

Den Hertog, J. Friso and Edward Huizenga. *The Knowledge Enterprise: Implementation of Intelligent Business Strategies.* London: Imperial College Press, 1999.

Deshpande, Rohit, ed. *Using Market Knowledge.* Thousand Oaks, CA: Sage Publications, 2000.

Devlin, Keith J. *Infosense: Turning Information into Knowledge.* New York: W.H. Freeman, 1999.

Dhar, Vasant and Roger Stein. *Intelligent Decision Support Methods: The Science of Knowledge Work.* New York: Prentice Hall College Division, 1997.

DiBella, Anthony J. and Edwin C. Nevis. *How Organizations Learn: An Integrated Strategy for Building Learning Capability.* San Francisco: Jossey-Bass Publishers, 1998.

Dillion, Patrick M. *The Quest for Knowledge Management: A New Service Organization to Address the Challenges & Opportunities. Technology Management Report, T-303.* Atlanta, GA: Information Management Forum, 1997.

Dixon, Nancy M. *Common Knowledge: How Companies Thrive by Sharing What They Know.* Boston: Harvard Business School Press, 2000.

Drucker, Peter F. *Innovation and Entrepreneurship: Practice and Principles.* New York: HarperBusiness, 1993.

Drucker, Peter F. *Management Challenges for the 21st Century.* Woburn, MA: Butterworth-Heinemann, 1999.

Drucker, Peter F. *Managing for the Future: The 1990s and Beyond.* New York: Truman Tally Books, 1992.

Drucker, Peter F. *Managing in a Time of Great Change.* New York: Truman Tally Books, 1995.

Drucker, Peter Ferdinand and Jacques Chaize. *Le Knowledge Management.* Paris: Ed. d'Organisation, l'Expansion Management Review, 1999.

Duff, Carolyn S. *Learning From Other Women: How to Benefit From the Knowledge, Wisdom, and Experience of Female Mentors.* New York: AMACOM, 1999.

Duffy, Jan. *Harvesting Experience: Reaping the Benefits of Knowledge.* Prairie Village, KS: ARMA International, 1999.

Duncan, William R. *A Guide to the Project Management Body of Knowledge.* Ambler, PA: Project Management Institute Publications, 1996.

Dutrénit, Gabriela. *Learning and Knowledge Management in the Firm: From Knowledge Accumulation to Strategic Capabilities.* Northampton, MA: Edward Elgar Publishing, 2000.

Dymsza, William A. and Robert G. Vambery, eds. *International Business Knowledge.* New York: Praeger Publishing, 1986.

Eden, Colin and J. C. Spender, eds. *Managerial and Organizational Cognition: Theory, Methods and Research.* London: Sage Publications, 1998.

Edvinsson, Leif and Michael S. Malone. *Intellectual Capital: Realizing Your Company's True Value by Finding Its Hidden Roots.* New York: HarperBusiness, 1997.

Ehin, Charles Kalev, Ph.D. *Unleashing Intellectual Capital.* Woburn, MA: Butterworth-Heinemann, Ltd., 2000.

Ekstedt, Eskil et al., eds. *Neo-Industrial Organizing: Renewal by Action and Knowledge Formation in a Project-Intensive Economy.* New York: Routledge, 1999.

Elaisson, Gunnar. *Firm Objectives, Controls, and Organization: The Use of Information and the Tranfer of Knowledge within the Firm.* Boston: Kluwer Publishing, 1996.

Empires of the Mind: Lessons to Lead and Succeed in a Knowledge-Based World. New York: William Morrow, 1995.

Enos, John. *The Creation of Technological Capability in Developing Countries.* London: Pinter, 1991.

Ernst & Young CBI. *Executives Perspectives on Knowledge in the Organization.* Boston: Ernst & Young Center for Business Innovation and Intelligence, 1997.

Evans, Phillip and Thomas S. Wurster. *Blown to Bits: How the New Economics of Information Transforms Strategy.* Boston: Harvard Business School Press, 1999.

Fahey, Liam and Robert M. Randall, eds. *Learning from the Future: Competitive Foresight Scenarios.* New York: John Wiley & Sons, 1998.

Faulkner, Wendy and Jacqueline Senker. *Knowledge Frontiers: Public Sector Research and Industrial Innovation in Biotechnology, Engineering Ceramics, and Parallel Computing.* Oxford: Clarendon Press, 1995.

Fayyad, Usama et al., eds. *Advances in Knowledge Discovery and Data Mining.* Cambridge, MA: MIT Press, 1996.

Feltovich, Paul et al., eds. *Expertise in Content.* Cambridge, MA: MIT Press, 1997.

Ferratt, Thomas and Ritu Agarwal. *Coping with Labor Scarcity in Information Technology.* Cincinnati, OH: Pinnaflex Educational Resources, Inc., 1999.

Fiddis, Christine. *Managing Knowledge in the Supply Chain: The Key to Competitive Advantage.* London: Financial Times Retail & Consumer, 1998.

Fincham, Robert, ed. *New Relationships in the Organised Professions: Mangers, Professionals and Knowledge Workers.* London: Avebury, 1997.

Finin, Timothy W. et al. *Information and Knowledge Management: Expanding the Definition of 'Database': First International Conference CIKM '92, Baltimore, Maryland, USA.* Berlin: Springer-Verlag, 1993.

Fischer, Laura. *Excellence in Practice Volume III: Innovation & Excellence in Workflow Process and Knowledge Management.* Lighthouse Point: Future Strategies, 2000.

Firlej, Maureen. *Knowledge Elicitation.* Upper Saddle River, NJ: Prentice Hall, 1990.

Fisher, Kimball and Maureen Duncan Fisher. *The Distributed Mind: Achieving High Performance Through the Collective Intelligence of Knowledge Work Teams.* New York: AMACOM, 1998.

Forrest, Andrew. *50 Ways Toward a Learning Organisation.* London: Industrial Society, 1999.

Friedman, Ken. *Individual Knowledge in the Information Society.* Sandvika, Norway: Norwegian School of Management, 1996.

Fruin, W. Mark. *Knowledge Works: Managing Intellectual Capital at Toshiba.* New York: Oxford University Press, 1997.

Funes, Mariana and Nancy Johnson. *Honing Your Knowledge Skills: A Route Map.* Woburn, MA: Butterworth-Heinemann, 1998.

Gaines, Brian, ed. *Artificial Intelligence in Knowledge Management: Papers from the 1997 Spring Symposium.* Menlo Park, CA: AAAI Press, 1997.

Gamble, Rose, ed. *Using AI for Knowledge Management & Business Process Reengineering: Papers from the AAAI Workshop.* Menlo Park, CA: AAAI Press, 1998.

Ganguly, Ashok S. *Business Driven Research and Development: Managing Knowledge to Create Wealth.* Houndmills, Basingstoke, Hampshire: Macmillan, 1999.

Gates, Bill and Collins Hemingway. *Business @ the Speed of Thought Using a Digital Nervous System.* New York: Warner Books, 1999.

Geisler, Eliezer. *Methodology, Theory, and Knowledge in the Managerial and Organizational Sciences.* Westport, CT: Quorum Books, 1999.

Gibson, Cyrus F. and Barbara B. Jackson. *The Information Imperative: Managing the Impact of Information Technology on Business and People.* Lexington, MA: D.C. Heath, 1987.

Gillespie, Richard. *Manufacturing Knowledge: A History of the Hawthorne Experiments.* Cambridge: Cambridge University Press, 1993.

Gladstone, Bryan. *From Know-How to Knowledge: The Essential Guide to Understanding and Implementing Knowledge Management.* London: Industrial Society, 2000.

Glasson, B. et al., eds. *The International Office of the Future.* New York: Chapman & Hall, 1996.

Glewwe, Paul et al. *Textbooks and Test Scores: Evidence from a Prospective Evaluation in Kenya.* Washington, DC: Development Research Group, World Bank, 1997.

Gonzalez, Jennifer Stone. *The 21st Century Intranet.* Upper Saddle River, NJ: Prentice Hall PTR, 1997.

Gray, H. M. *Warfighting: The US Marine Corps Book of Strategy.* New York: Doubleday, 1989.

Grossman, Evan. *Knowledge Management Technologies: Perspectives on Recent Trends and Their Implications.* Lexington, MA: Nextera Enterprises L.L.C., 1998.

Grossman, Evan and Dawne Shand. *Trends in Knowledge Management Techniques.* Lexington, MA: Nextera Enterprises L.L.C., 1998.

Gundry, John R. and George Metes. *Agile Networking: Competing through the Internet and Intranets.* Upper Saddle River, NJ: Prentice Hall PTR, 1997.

Hackett, Brian. *Beyond Knowledge Management: New Ways to Work and Learn.* New York: Conference Board, 2000.

Hackett, Brian. *Managing Knowledge: The HR Role.* New York: Conference Board, 1999.

Hackett, Brian. *The Value of Training in the Era of Intellectual Capital: A Research Report. Conference Board Report, 1199-97-RR.* New York: Conference Board, 1997.

Hadley, Laura et al. *Strategic Knowledge Management: An In-Depth Examination of the Data Warehouse and Data Mining Industry.* Phoenix, AZ: Applied Computer Research, Inc., 1999.

Halal, William E., ed. and Raymond W. Smith. *The Infinite Resource: Creating and Managing the Knowledge Enterprise*. San Francisco: Jossey-Bass Publishers, 1998.

Hammergren, Tom. *Data Warehousing: Building the Corporate Knowledge*. London: International Thomson Publishing, 1997.

Hanson, T. and J. Day. *Managing the Electronic Library*. Munich: Bowker-Saur, 1999.

Harris, K. *Why Knowledge Management Is in Your Future: Document BPR SPA-KM-280*. New York: Gartner Group, 1997.

Harryson, Sigvald. *Japanese Technology and Innovation Management: From Know-How to Know-Who*. Northhampton, MA: Edward Elgar Publishing, 1998.

Harryson, Sigvald. *Managing Know-Who Based Companies: A Multinetworked Approach to Knowledge and Innovation Management*. Cheltenham: Edward Elgar Publications, 2000.

Harvard Business School. *Harvard Business Review on Knowledge Management*. Boston: Harvard Business School Press, 1998.

Haskell, Robert E. *Reengineering Corporate Training: Intellectual Capital and Transfer of Learning*. Westport, CT: Greenwood Publishing Group, 1998.

Haywood, Trevor. *Only Connect: Shaping Networks and Knowledge for the New Millenium*. East Grinstead: Bowker-Saur, 1999.

Henderson, Richard I. *Compensation Management in a Knowledge-Based World*. Upper Saddle River, NJ: Prentice Hall, 2000.

Heydorn, Barbara. *Technology Management Practices for Performance and Growth*. Menlo Park, CA: SRI Consulting Business Intelligence Program, 1998.

Hinrichs, Randy. *Intranets: What's the Bottom Line?* Upper Saddle River, NJ: Prentice Hall, 1997.

Hodge, Gail. *Systems of Knowledge Organization for Digital Libraries: Beyond Traditional Authority Files*. Washington, DC: Digital Library Federation, 2000.

Hofmann, Marcelo. *Change Forces in the Information Business*. Menlo Park, CA: SRI Consulting Business Intelligence Program, 1998.

Holeton, Richard. *Composing Cyberspace: Identity, Community, and Knowledge in the Electronic Age*. New York: McGraw-Hill College Division, 1997.

Holsapple, Clyde W. and Andrew B. Whinston. *The Information Jungle: A Quasi-Novel Approach to Knowledge Management*. New York: McGraw-Hill, 1998.

Holtshouse, Dan, ed. and Christopher Meyer. *The Knowledge Advantage: 14 Visionaries Define Marketplace Success in the New Economy.* Oxford: Capstone, Ltd., 1999.

Holtshouse, Dan and Rudy Ruggles. *The Knowledge Advantage: Leveraging Knowledge into Marketplace Success.* Oxford: Capstone Publishing, 1999.

Honeycutt, Jerry. *Evaluating Knowledge Management Solutions.* New York: Little, Brown, 2000.

Honeycutt, Jerry, Jr. *Knowledge Management Strategies.* Seattle: Microsoft Press, 2000.

Horibe, Frances Dale Emy. *Managing Knowledge Workers: New Skills and Attitudes to Unlock the Intellectual Capital in Your Organization.* Toronto: John Wiley & Sons, 1999.

Horvath, J. A. et al. *Tacit Knowledge in Military Leadership: Evidence from Officer Interviews, Technical Report 1018.* Alexandria, VA: U.S. Army Research Institute for the Behavioral and Social Sciences, 1994.

Horvath, J. A. et al. *Tacit Knowledge for Military Leadership: Some Research Products and Their Applications to Leadership Development.* Alexandria, VA: US Army Research Institute, 1998.

Horvath, J. A. et al. *Tacit Knowledge in Military Leadership: Supporting Instrument Development, Technical Report 1042.* Alexandria, VA: U.S. Army Research Institute for the Behavioral and Social Sciences, 1996.

Huang, Kuan-Tsae et al. *Quality Information and Knowledge.* Upper Saddle River, NJ: Prentice Hall PTR, 1999.

Hudson, William J. *Intellectual Capital: How to Build It, Enhance It, Use It.* New York: John Wiley & Sons, 1993.

Huff, A. S., ed. *Mapping Strategic Thought.* Chichester, NY: John Wiley & Sons, 1990.

Huseman, Richard C. *Leading the Knowledge: The Nature of Competition in the 21st Century.* Thousand Oaks, CA: Sage Publications, 1999.

Huseman, Richard C. and Jon P. Goodman. *Leading with Knowledge: Winning in the Realm of the Red Queen.* London: Sage Publications, 1998.

Imparato, Nicholas. *Capital for Our Time: The Economic, Legal, and Management Challenges of Intellectual Capital.* Stanford, CA: Hoover Institution Press, 1999.

Information and Knowledge Management. Berlin: Springer-Verlag, 1993.

The Information Revolution and the Future of Telecommunications. Washington, DC: World Bank, 1997.

Inmon, William H. et al. *Data Stores, Data Warehousing and the Zachman Framework: Managing Enterprise Knowledge.* New York: Computing McGraw-Hill, 1997.

Intellectual Capital Core Asset for the Third Millennium Enterprise. London: International Thomson Business Press, 1996.

Jacques, Roy. *Manufacturing the Employee: Knowledge Management from the 19th to 21st Centuries.* London: Sage Publications, 1996.

Jeffcutt, Paul. *The Foundations of Management Knowledge: Examining Complex Relations Between Theory and Practice.* London: Routledge, 2000.

Jonassen, D. et al. *Explicit Methods for Conveying Structural Knowledge through Concept Maps.* Hillsdale, NJ: Lawrence Erlbaum Associates, 1993.

Kafai, Yasmin and Mitchell Resnick, eds. *Constructionism in Practice: Designing, Thinking and Learning in a Digital World.* Hillsdale, NJ: Lawrence Erlbaum Associates, 1996.

Kelly, Kevin. *New Rules for the New Economy: 10 Radical Strategies for a Connected World.* New York: Viking Press, 1998.

Kerchner, Charles Taylor et al. *United Mind Workers: Unions and Teaching in the Knowledge Society.* San Francisco: Jossey-Bass Publishers, 1997.

Kerr, Roger M. *Knowledge-Based Manufacturing Management: Applications of Artificial Intelligence to the Effective Management of Manufacturing Companies.* Reading, MA: Addison Wesley Publishing Co., 1991.

Kingma, B. *The Economics of Information: A Guide to Economic and Cost-Benefit Analysis* Englewood, CO: Libraries Unlimited, 1996.

Kirby, J. Philip and David Hughes. *Thoughtware: Change the Thinking and the Organization Will Change Itself.* Cambridge: Productivity Press, 1997.

Kirn, S. and Gregory O'Hare, eds. *Cooperative Knowledge Processing: The Key Technology for Intelligent Organizations.* Berlin: Springer-Verlag, 1997.

Klein, David A., ed. *The Strategic Management of Intellectual Capital. Resources for the Knowledge-Based Economy.* Woburn, MA: Butterworth-Heinemann, 1998.

Knight, Tom. *Knowledge Management for IT Professionals.* Woburn, MA: Butterworth-Heinemann.

Knowledge Management: A Competitive Asset. Washington, DC: Special Libraries Association, 1998.

Knowledge Management at Hewlett-Packard, KM34. Chapel Hill, NC: Best Practices LLC, 2000.

Knowledge Management in the Innovation Process. Washington, DC: Industrial Research Institute, 1999.

Knowledge Management: Knowledge Management Promise and Reality. Boston: Delphi Group, 1998.

Koulopoulos, Thomas M. *Smart Things to Know about Knowledge Management.* Oxford: Capstone Publishing, 1999.

Koulopoulos, Tom M. *Knowledge Management.* Oxford: Capstone Publishing, 1999.

Kruschwitz, Nina and George Lothar Roth. *Inventing Organizations of the 21st Century: Producing Knowledge through Collaboration.* Cambridge, MA: Center for Coordination Science, Massachusetts Institute of Technology, Sloan School of Management, 1999.

Latour, Bruno. *Aramis, or, The Love of Technology.* Boston: Harvard University Press, 1996.

Lazega, Emmanuel. *The Micropolitics of Knowledge: Communication and Indirect Control in Workgroups.* Berlin: de Gruyter, 1992.

Leidner, Dorothy E. *Understanding Information Culture: Integrating Knowledge Management Systems into Organizations.* Fontainebleau: INSEAD, 1998.

Leonard-Barton, Dorothy. *Wellsprings of Knowledge: Building and Sustaining the Sources of Innovation.* Boston: Harvard Business School Press, 1995.

Lepore, Domenico and Oded Cohen. *Deming and Goldratt: The Theory of Constraints and the System of Profound Knowledge.* Great Barrington, MA: North River Press, 1999.

Lesk, M. *Practical Digital Libraries.* San Francisco: Morgan Kaufmann, 1997.

Lesser, Eric. *Knowledge and Social Capital, Foundations and Applications.* Woburn, MA: Butterworth-Heinemann, 2000.

Lesser, Eric et al. *Knowledge and Communities.* Woburn, MA: Butterworth-Heinemann, 2000.

Levine, J. et al. *Shared Cognition in-Organizations: The Management of Knowledge.* Hillsdale, NJ: Lawrence Erlbaum Associates, 1999.

Liebenau, Lee A. J. and J. De Gross, eds. *Qualitative Method in Information Systems.* New York: Chapman & Hall, 1997.

Liebowitz, Jay. *Building Organizational Intelligence: A Knowledge Management Primer.* Boca Raton, FL: CRC Press, 1999.

Liebowitz, Jay. *Information Technology Management: A Knowledge Repository.* Boca Raton, FL: CRC Press, 1999.

Liebowitz, Jay, ed. *Knowledge Management Handbook.* Boca Raton, FL: CRC Press, 1999.

Liebowitz, Jay and Tom Beckman. *Knowledge Organizations: What Every Manager Should Know.* Boca Raton, FL: St. Lucie Press, 1998.

Liebowitz, Jay and Lyle C. Wilcox, eds. *Knowledge Management and Its Integrative Elements.* Boca Raton, FL: CRC Press, 1997.

Line, Maurice et al., eds. *Library and Information Work Worldwide: 1998.* London: Bowker-Saur, 1998.

Liu, H. J. and H. Motoda. *KDD: Techniques and Applications: 23-24 February 1997: Proceedings of the First Pacific-Asia Conference on Knowledge Discovery and Data Mining.* Singapore: World Scientific Publishing Co., 1997.

Liu, Huan and Hiroshi Motoda. *Feature Selection for Knowledge Discovery and Data Mining.* Woburn, MA: Kluwer Academic Publishing, 1998.

Lloyd, Peter and Paula Boyle. *Web-Weaving: Intranets, Extranets and Strategic Alliances.* Woburn, MA: Butterworth-Heinemann, 1998.

Loshin, David. *Enterprise Knowledge Management: The Data Quality Approach.* San Francisco: Morgan Kaufmann, 2000.

Machlup, Fritz. *The Economics of Information and Human Capital.* Princeton, NJ: Princeton University Press, 1980.

Machlup, Fritz. *Knowledge and Knowledge Production.* Princeton, NJ: Princeton University Press, 1980.

Machlup, Fritz. *Knowledge: Its Creation, Distribution and Significance.* Princeton, NJ: Princeton University Press, 1980.

Magretta, Joan, ed. *Managing in the New Economy.* Boston: Harvard Business School Press, 1999.

Malhotra, Yogesh, ed. *Knowledge Management & Virtual Organizations.* Hershey, PA: Idea Group Publishing, 2000.

Malone, Samuel A. *How to Set Up and Manage a Corporate Learning Centre.* Aldershot, VT: Gower, 1997.

Managing Intellectual Capital for Strategic Advantage. Henley-on-Thames: Henley Management College, 1996.

Mann, Jim. *Tomorrow's Global Community: How the Information Deluge Is Transforming Business & Government.* Philadelphia: Bainbridge Books, 1998.

Mansell, Robin and Uta Wehn. *Knowledge Societies: Information Technology for Sustainable Development.* New York: Oxford University Press, 1998.

March, Artemis. *A Note on Knowledge Management.* Boston: Harvard Business School, 1997.

March, James G. *The Pursuit of Organizational Intelligence.* Oxford: Blackwell Publishing, 1999.

Marchand, Don. *Competing with Information: Unleashing Corporate Knowledge for Competitive Advantage.* Chichester, NY: John Wiley & Sons, 2000.

Marchand, Don. *The Informed Company.* Harlow: Financial Times Prentice Hall, 2000.

Marquardt, Michael J. and Greg Kearsley. *Technology-Based Learning: Maximizing Human Performance and Corporate Success.* Boca Raton, FL: CRC Press, 1999.

Matarazzo, James M. and Suzanne D. Connolly. *Knowledge and Special Libraries.* Woburn, MA: Butterworth-Heinemann, 1999.

Matthews, Monte Lee. *Knowledge-Driven Profit Improvement.* Boca Raton, FL: CRC Press, 1999.

Mattison, Rob and Brigitte Kilger-Mattison. *Web Warehousing and Knowledge Management.* New York: McGraw-Hill, 1999.

Mattos, Nelson Mendonca. *An Approach to Knowledge-Based Management.* Berlin: Springer-Verlag, 1991.

Maule, R. William. *Information, Communications & Technology in Organizations: An Introduction to Information Studies, Informatics & Knowledge Management.* San Francisco: Information Associates Press, 1999.

McCall, Nancy and Lisa A. Mix, eds. *Designing Archival Programs to Advance Knowledge in the Health Fields.* Baltimore: Johns Hopkins University Press, 1995.

McGee, James V. et al. *Managing Information Strategically.* New York: John Wiley & Sons, 1993.

McGonagle, J. J. and C. M. Vella. *Outsmarting the Competition: Practical Approaches to Finding and Using Competitive Information.* Naperville, IL: Sourcebooks, 1990.

McGregor, Eugene B. *Strategic Management of Human Knowledge, Skills, and Abilities: Workforce Decision Making in the Post-Industrial Era.* San Francisco: Jossey-Bass Publishers, 1991.

McInerney, Claire R. *Providing Data, Information, and Knowledge to the Virtual Office: Organizational Support for Remote Workers.* Washington, DC: Special Libraries Association, 1999.

McKinnon, Sharon M. and William J. Bruns. *The Information Mosaic.* Boston: Harvard Business School Press, 1992.

McWhinney, Will. *Paths of Change: Strategic Choices for Organizations and Society.* Thousand Oaks, CA: Sage Publications, 1997.

Merlyn, Paul R. *From IT to KT—But Don't Forget the User.* Menlo Park, CA: SRI Consulting Business Intelligence Program, 1998.

Meyer, W. *Expert Systems in Factory Management: Knowledge-Based CIM.* Chichester: Ellis Horwood, Ltd., 1990.

Middleton, D., and D. Edwards, eds. *Collective Remembering.* Newbury Park: Sage, 1990.

Miles, M. B. and M. A. Huberman. *Qualitative Data Analysis, An Expanded Sourcebook.* Beverly Hills, CA: Sage, 1994.

Miller, Jerry, ed. *Millenium Intelligence: Understanding & Conducting Competitive Intelligence in the Digital Age.* Medford, NJ: CyberAge Books, 2000.

Miller, William F. *Crafting and Coaching Intellectual Organizations.* Minneapolis, MN: Center for the Development of Technological Leadership Institute of Technology University of Minnesota, 1989.

Miller, William L. and Langdon Morris. *Fourth Generation R & D: Managing Knowledge, Technology, and Innovation.* New York: John Wiley & Sons, 1999.

Milner, Eileen. *Managing Information and Knowledge in the Public Sector.* London: Routledge, 2000.

Mohr, L. B. *Explaining Organizational Behavior.* San Francisco: Jossey-Bass Publishers, 1982.

Mohrman, Susan Albers et al. *Designing Team-Based Organizations: New Forms for Knowledge Work.* San Francisco: Jossey-Bass Publishers, 1995.

Moingeon, Bertrand and Amy C. Edmondson, eds. *Organizational Learning and Competitive Advantage.* Thousand Oaks, CA: Sage Publications, 1996.

Morey, Daryl et al., eds. *Knowledge Management: Classic & Contemporary Works.* Cambridge, MA: MIT Press, 2000.

Morris, Stephen. *The Knowledge Manager: Adding Value in the Information Age.* London: Pitman, 1996.

Morris, Steve et al. *The Knowledge Manager.* London: Financial Times Management, 1997.

Murdoch, S. and L. Johnson. *Intelligent Data Handling.* New York: Chapman & Hall, 1990.

Myers, Paul S., ed. *Knowledge Management and Organizational Design. Resources for the Knowledge-Based Economy.* Woburn, MA: Butterworth-Heinemann, 1996.

Neef, Dale, ed. *The Knowledge Economy: Resources for the Knowledge-Based Economy.* Woburn, MA: Butterworth-Heinemann, 1998.

Neef, Dale. *A Little Knowledge Is a Dangerous Thing: Understanding Our Global Knowledge Economy.* Woburn, MA: Butterworth-Heinemann, 1998.

Newman, Amy. *Knowledge Management.* Alexandria, VA: American Society for Training & Development, 1999.

Niwa, Kiyoshi. *Knowledge-Based Risk Management in Engineering: A Case Study in Human-Computer Cooperative Systems.* New York: John Wiley & Sons, 1989.

Nonaka, Ikujiro and Toshihiro Nishiguchi. *Knowledge and Emergence: Social, Technical, and Evolutionary Dimensions of Knowledge Creation.* New York: Oxford University Press, 2000.

Nonaka, Ikujiro and Hirotaka Takeuchi. *The Knowledge-Creating Company: How Japanese Companies Create the Dynamics of Innovation.* New York: Oxford University Press, 1995.

Nordhaug, Odd. *Human Capital in Organizations: Competence, Training, and Learning.* Oslo: Scandinavian University Press, 1994.

North, Klaus. *Localizing Global Production.* Geneva: ILO, 1998.

O'Dell, Carla S. et al. *If Only We Knew What We Knew: The Transfer of Internal Knowledge and Best Practice.* New York: Free Press, 1998.

Papows, Jeff. *Enterprise.com: Market Leadership in the Information Age.* Reading, MA: Perseus Books, 1998.

Pareschi, Remo and B. Fronhofer, eds. *From the Frame Problems to Knowledge Management.* Boston: Kluwer Academic Publishing, 1999.

Parker, Marilyn M. *Strategic Transformation and Information Technology.* Upper Saddle River, NJ: Prentice Hall, 1995.

Pasternack, Bruce A. and Albert J. Viscio. *The Centerless Corporation: Transforming Your Organization for Growth & Prosperity in the New Millennium.* New York: S & S Trade, 1998.

Pau, Louis F. and Claudio Gianotti. *Economic and Financial Knowledge-Based Processing.* Berlin: Springer-Verlag, 1990.

Pearce, Robert D. *Global Competition and Technology: Essays in the Creation and Application of Knowledge by Multinationals.* New York: St. Martin's Press, 1997.

Pepper, Jeff. *Smart Support: How to Transform Your Support Organization by Leveraging What You Know.* Oakmont, PA: ServiceWare, 1999.

Pfeffer, Jeffrey and Robert I. Sutton. *The Knowing-Doing Gap: How Smart Companies Turn Knowledge into Action.* Boston: Harvard Business School Press, 1999.

Pinelli, Thomas et al. *Knowledge Diffusion in the U. S. Aerospace Industry: Managing Knowledge for Competitive Advantage.* Norwood, NJ: Ablex Publishing Corp., 1998.

Plant, Richard E. and Nicholas D. Stone. *Knowledge Based Systems in Agriculture*. New York: McGraw-Hill Text, 1991.

Polanyi, Michael. *The Tacit Dimension*. Garden City, NY: Doubleday Anchor, 1966.

Polanyi, Michael. *Tacit Knowledge*. New York: Doubleday, 1966.

Polanyi, Michael. *Personal Knowledge: Towards a Post-Critical Philosophy*. London: Routledge, 1973.

Popkewitz, Thomas S., ed. *Educational Knowledge: Changing Relationships between the State, Civil Society, and the Educational Community*. Albany, NY: State University of New York Press, 2000.

Porac, Joseph Francis Allen and Raghu Garud. *Cognition, Knowledge and Organizations*. Stamford, CT: JAI Press, 1999.

Porter, Michael E. *Competitive Advantage: Creating and Sustaining Superior Performance*. New York: Free Press, 1998.

Porter, Michael E. *Competitive Strategy: Techniques for Analyzing Industries and Competitors*. New York: Free Press, 1998.

Pouliquen, Louis Y. *Rural Infrastructure from a World Bank Perspective: A Knowledge Management Framework*. Washington, DC: World Bank, 1999.

Prange, Christiane. *Managing Business Networks: An Inquiry into Managerial Knowledge in the Multimedia Industry*. Frankfurt: Peter Lang Publishing, 1999.

Prescott, J. E. and P. T. Gibbons, eds. *Global Perspectives on Competitive Intelligence*. Alexandria, VA: Society of Competitive Intelligence Professionals, 1993.

Probst, Gilbert. *Managing Knowledge: Building Blocks for Success*. Chichester, NY: John Wiley & Sons, 1999.

Probst, Gilbert et al. *Managing Knowledge. How Companies Use Their Most Valuable Resource*. (German) Frankfurt: Frankfurter Allgemeine Zeitung, 1998.

Prusak, Laurence, ed. *Knowledge in Organizations. Resources for the Knowledge-Based Economy*. Woburn, MA: Butterworth-Heinemann, 1997.

Puckett, J. M. and H. W. Reese, eds. *Mechanisms of Everyday Cognition*. Hillsdale, NJ: Lawrence Erlbaum Associates, 1993.

Quinn, James Brian. *Intelligent Enterprise: A Knowledge and Service Based Paradigm for Industry*. New York: Free Press, 1992.

Quinn, James Brian et al. *Innovation Explosion: Using Intellect and Software to Revolutionize Growth Strategies*. New York: Free Press, 1997.

Radding, Alan. *Knowledge Mangement: Succeeding in the Information-Based Global Economy*. Portland, OR: Computer Research Technology Corp., 1998.

Reber, A. S. *Implicit Learning and Tacit Knowledge: An Essay on the Cognitive Unconscious*. New York: Oxford University Press, 1993.

Reisman, Arnold. *Management Science Knowledge: Its Creation, Generalization, and Consolidation*. Westport, CT: Greenwood Publishing Group, 1992.

Richardson, John V., Jr. *Knowledge-Based Systems for General Reference Work: Applications, Problems, and Progress*. San Diego: Academic Press, 1995.

Roos, Johan, ed. *Intellectual Capital: Navigating in the New Business Landscape*. New York: New York University Press, 1998.

Roos, Johan and Georg von Krogh, eds. *Organizational Epistemology*. New York: Macmillan, 1995.

Rowe, Alan J. and Sue Anne Davis. *Intelligent Information Systems: Meeting the Challenge of the Knowledge Era*. Westport, CT: Quorum Books, 1996.

Ruggles, Rudy. *The Knowledge Advantage: Leveraging Knowledge into Marketplace Success*. Oxford: Capstone Publishing, 1999.

Ruggles, Rudy L., ed. *Knowledge Management Tools. Resources of the Knowledge-Based Economy*. Woburn, MA: Butterworth-Heinemann, 1997.

Saffady, William. *Knowledge Management: A Manager's Briefing*. Prairie Village, KS: ARMA International, 1998.

Salazar, Yolanda L. and Emily A. Cullen. *Common Knowledge: When You File It, Can You Find It?* A. D. A. P. T. Publishing Co., 1991.

Sanchez, Ron and Aimae Heene, eds. *Strategic Learning and Knowledge Management*. New York, NY: John Wiley & Sons, 1997.

Saunders, Laverna, ed. *The Evolving Virtual Library II: Practical and Philosophical Perspectives*. Medford, NJ: Information Today, 1999.

Savage, Charles M. *Fifth Generation Management: Co-Creating Through Virtual Enterprising, Dynamic Teaming, and Knowledge Networking*. Woburn, MA: Butterworth-Heinemann, 1996.

Savage, Charles M. *Fifth Generation Management: Integrating Enterprises Through Human Networking*. Bedford, MA: Digital Press, 1990.

Scarbrough, Harry. *Knowledge Management: A Literature Review*. London: Institute of Personnel and Development, 1999.

Schmidt, Joachim W. and Constantino Thanos. *Foundations of Knowledge Management: Contribution from Logic, Databases, and Artificial Intelligence*. Berlin: Springer-Verlag, 1989.

Schmidt, Stephen R. *Knowledge Based Management: Unleashing the Power of Quality Improvement.* Colorado Springs, CO: Air Academy Press, 1999.

Schneier, Bruce. *Applied Cryptography.* New York: John Wiley & Sons, 1996.

Schrage, M. *No More Teams! Mastering the Dynamics of Creative Collaboration.* New York: Currency/Doubleday, 1995.

Schreiber, Anne. *Knowledge Engineering and Management: The Commonkads Methodology.* Cambridge, MA: MIT Press, 1999.

Schwartz, David G. et al., eds. *Internet-Based Organizational Memory and Knowledge Management.* Hershey, PA: Idea Group Publishing, 2000.

Senge, Peter M. *The Fifth Discipline Fieldbook: Strategies and Tools for Building a Learning Organization.* New York: Doubleday/Currency, 1994.

Senge, Peter M. *The Fifth Discipline: The Art and Practice of the Learning Organization.* New York: Doubleday/Currency, 1990.

Seybold, Patricia B. *Customers.Com: How to Create a Profitable Business Strategy for the Internet and Beyond.* New York: Times Books, 1998.

Shapiro, Carl and Hal R. Varian. *Information Rules: A Strategic Guide to the Network Economy.* Boston: Harvard Business School Press, 1998.

Shenai, Krishna. *Introduction to Database and Knowledge-Base Systems.* Singapore: World Scientific Publishing Co., 1992.

Shukla, Madhukar. *Competing Through Knowledge: Building a Learning Organization.* Thousand Oaks, CA: Sage India Private, 1997.

Shulman, Seth. *Owning the Future.* Boston: Houghton Mifflin, 1999.

Sigismund, Charles G. *The Knowledge Masters: Visionary Thinking from the Champions of Silicon Valley.* New York: John Wiley & Sons, 2000.

Sink, D. Scott et al. *By What Method Are You Developing the Knowledge and Skills to Lead Large-Scale Quality and Productivity Improvement?* Norcross, GA: Engineering & Management Press, 1997.

Skyrme, David. *Knowledge Networking: Creating the Collaborative Company.* Woburn, MA: Butterworth-Heinemann, 1998.

Slemko, Janet K. *MindWealth: Turning Knowledge into Assets.* Del Mar, CA: Career Research Institute, 1999.

Slywotzky, Adrian J. et al. *Profit Patterns: 30 Ways to Anticipate and Profit from Strategic Forces Reshaping Your Business.* New York: Random House, 1999.

Slywotzky, Adrian J. *The Profit Zone: How Strategic Business Design Will Lead You to Tomorrow's Profits.* New York: Times Books, 1998.

Smallman, Clive. *Knowledge Management as Risk Management: The Need for Open Corporate Governance*. Bradford: University of Bradford Management Centre, 1999.

Smallwood, Robert. *Managing Knowledge in a Paper World: How Document Technologies Enable Knowledge Management*. Woburn, MA: Butterworth-Heinemann, 2000.

Smith, David E. and David Elliott. *Knowledge, Groupware, and the Internet*. Woburn, MA: Butterworth-Heinemann, 1999.

Sonnenreich, Wes and Tim Macinta. *Web Developer.Com® Guide to Search Engines*. New York: John Wiley & Sons, 1998.

Sparrow, John. *Knowledge in Organizations: Access to Thinking at Work*. London: Sage Publications, 1998.

Special Libraries Association Staff. *Knowledge Management: A New Competitive Asset*. Washington, DC: Special Libraries Association, 1998.

Spitzer, Quinn and Ron Evans. *Heads You Win! How the Best Companies Think*. New York: Simon and Schuster, 1997.

Spurge, Lorraine, ed. *Knowledge Exchange Business Encyclopedia, Illustrated*. Santa Monica, CA: Knowledge Exchange, 1995.

Srikantaiah, Kanti and Michael E. D. Koenig, eds. *Knowledge Management for the Information Professional*. Medford, NJ: Information Today, 1999.

Starkey, Ken, ed. *How Organizations Learn*. London: International Thomson Business Press, 1996.

State of Wyoming Information Technology Strategic Plan. Cheyenne, WY: State of Wyoming, 1998.

Stern, David, ed. *Digital Libraries: Philosophies, Technical Design Considerations and Example Scenarios*. Binghamton, NY: Haworth Press, 1999.

Sternberg, Robert and Joseph Horvath, eds. *Tacit Knowledge in Professional Practice*. Hillsdale, NJ: Lawrence Erlbaum Associates, 1998.

Stewart, Thomas A. *Intellectual Capital: How the Knowledge Economy Is Creating New Challenges for Corporations & New Opportunities for the People Who Work for Them*. New York: Doubleday, 1997.

Stewart, Thomas A. *Intellectual Capital: The New Wealth of Organizations*. New York: Doubleday/Currency, 1997.

Stielow, Frederick, ed. *Creating a Virtual Library: A How-to-Do-It Manual*. New York: Neal-Schuman Publishers, 1999.

Sullivan, Patrick H., ed. *Profiting from Intellectual Capital: Extracting Value from Innovation*. New York: John Wiley & Sons, 1998.

Sullivan, Patrick H. *Value-Driven Intellectual Capital: How to Convert Intangible Corporate Assets into Market Value.* New York: John Wiley & Sons, 2000.

Sveiby, Karl Erik. *The New Organizational Wealth: Mangaging & Measuring Knowledge-Based Assets.* San Francisco: Berrett-Koehler Publishers, 1997.

Swan, Jacky and Harry Scarbrough. *Case Studies in Knowledge Management.* London: Institute of Personnel Management, 1999.

Swanstrom, Edward. *Knowledge Management: Modelling and Managing the Knowledge Process.* New York: John Wiley & Sons, 1999.

Swanstrom, Edward. *Knowledge Management Using Object-Oriented Change & Learning.* New York: John Wiley & Sons, 2000.

Synnott, W. R. and W. H. Gruber. *Information Resource Management: Opportunities and Strategies for the 1980s.* New York: John Wiley & Sons, 1980.

Talero, Eduardo and Philip Gaudette. *Harnessing Information for Development: World Bank Group Vision and Strategy, Draft Document.* Washington, DC: The World Bank, 1995.

Tansley, D. S. W. and C. C. Hayball. *Knowledge-Based Systems and Design.* New York: Prentice Hall, 1993.

Tecker, Glenn H. et al. *Building a Knowledge-Based Culture: Using Twenty-First Century Work and Decision-Making Systems in Associations.* Washington, DC: American Society of Association Executives, 1997.

Teece, David J. *Managing Intellectual Capital: Organizational, Strategic, and Policy Dimensions.* London: Oxford University Press, 2000.

Thierauf, Robert J. *Knowledge Management Systems for Business.* Westport, CT: Quorum Books, 1999.

Thomas, Vinod et al. *Embracing the Power of Knowledge for a Sustainable Environment.* Washington, DC: World Bank, 1997.

Thompson, Leigh et al. *Shared Cognition in Organizations: The Management of Knowledge.* Hillsdale, NJ: Lawrence Erlbaum Associates, 1999.

Thurbin, Patrick J. *Leveraging Knowledge: The 17-Day Program for a Learning Organization.* London: Pitman Publishing, Ltd., 1995.

Thurow, Lester C. *Building Wealth: The New Rules for Individuals, Companies and Nations in a Knowledge-Based Economy.* New York: Harper Business, 1999.

Tidd, Joe, ed. *From Knowledge Management to Strategic Competence: Measuring Technological, Market and Organizational Innovation.* London: Imperial College Press, 2000.

Technological, Market and Organizational Innovation. London: Imperial College Press, 2000.

Tirosh, D., ed. *Implicit and Explicit Knowledge: An Educational Approach.* Norwood, NJ: Ablex Publishing Corp., 1994.

Tissen, Rene et al. *Creating the 21st Century Company: Knowledge Intensive, People Rich.* Reading, MA: Addison Wesley Publishing Co., 1998.

Tissen, Rene et al. *Value-Based Knowledge Management: Creating the 21st Century Company: Knowledge Intensive, People Rich.* Reading, MA: Addison Wesley Publishing Co., 1998.

Tisseyre, René-Charles. *Knowledge Management: Théorie et Pratique de la Gestion des Connaissances.* Paris: Hermès Science Publications, 1999.

Tiwana, A. *Knowledge Management Toolkit.* Upper Saddle River, NJ: Prentice Hall, 1999.

Tobin, Daniel R. *The Knowledge-Enabled Organization: Moving from 'Training' to 'Learning' to Meet Business Goals.* New York: AMACOM, 1998.

Tobin, Daniel R. *Transformational Learning: Renewing Your Company through Knowledge and Skills.* New York: John Wiley & Sons, 1996.

Toogood, Granville N. *The Inspired Executive: The Art of Leadership in the Age of Knowledge.* New York: McGraw-Hill: 1999.

Tordoir, Pieter P. *The Professional Knowledge Economy: The Management and Integration of Professional Services in Business Organizations.* Boston: Kluwer Academic Publishing, 1996.

Turban, Efraim and Jay Liebowitz, eds. *Managing Expert Systems.* Hershey, PA: Idea Group Publishing, 1990.

Tyden, Thomas. *Knowledge Interplay: User-Oriented Research Dissemination through Synthesis Pedagogics.* Philadelphia: Coronet Books, 1993.

Vasarhelyi, Miklos A. and Dan O'Leary, eds. *Artificial Intelligence in Accounting and Auditing: Knowledge Management and Value Creation.* Princeton, NJ: Markus Wiener, 2000.

Vella, C. M. and J. J. McGonagle. *Competitive Intelligence in the Computer Age.* New York: Quorum Books, 1987.

Vine, David. *Internet Business Intelligence: How to Build a Big Company System on a Small Company Budget.* Medford, NJ: CyberAge Books, 2000.

Von Krogh, Georg. *Knowing in Firms: Understanding, Managing and Measuring Knowledge.* Walnut Creek, CA: Altamira, 1999.

Von Krogh, Georg and Johan Roos. *Managing Knowledge: Perspectives on Cooperation and Competition.* London: Sage Publications, 1996.

Von Krogh, Georg and Johan Roos. *Organizational Epistemology.* New York: St. Martin's Press, 1995.

Von Krogh, Georg et al., eds. *Enabling Knowledge Creation.* Oxford: Oxford University Press, 2000.

Von Krogh, Georg et al., eds. *Understanding, Managing, and Measuring Knowledge.* London: Sage, 1998.

Waitley, Denis. *Empires of the Mind: Lessons to Lead and Succeed in a Knowledge-Based World.* New York: Quill, 1996.

Webb, Sylvia P. *Knowledge Management: Linchpin of Change: Some Practical Guidelines.* London: ASLIB, 1998.

Wiig, Karl M. *Knowledge Management.* Arlington, TX: Schema Press, 1995.

Wiig, Karl M. *Knowledge Management: The Central Focus for Intelligent-Acting Organizations.* Arlington, TX: Schema Press, 1994.

Wiig, Karl M. *Knowledge Management Foundations: Thinking About Thinking How People and Organizations Represent, Create and Use Knowledge.* Arlington, TX: Schema Press, 1993.

Wiig, Karl M. *Knowledge Management Methods: Practical Approaches to Managing Knowledge.* Arlington, TX: Schema Press, 1995.

Williams, M. E., ed. *Annual Review of Information Science and Technology. Vol. 30.* Medford, NJ: Information Today Inc., 1995.

Wills, Gordon. *The Knowledge Game: The Revolution in Learning and Communication in the Workplace.* London: Cassell Academic, 1998.

Wilson, David. *Managing Knowledge.* Woburn, MA: Butterworth-Heinemann, 1996.

Winslow, Charles D. and William L. Bramer. *FutureWork: Putting Knowledge to Work in the Knowledge Economy.* New York: Free Press, 1994.

Winter, Sidney G. and Oliver E. Williamson, eds. *The Nature of the Firm: Origins, Evolution, and Development.* Oxford: Oxford University Press, 1994.

Woods, Eric. *Knowledge Management: Applications, Markets and Technologies.* London: Ovum, 1998.

Woods, John A. and James W. Cortada. *Knowledge Management Yearbook 1999-2000.* Woburn, MA: Butterworth-Heinemann, 1999.

World Bank. *Assessing Aid, What Works, What Doesn't and Why.* Oxford: Oxford University Press, 1998.

Wriston, Walter B. *The Twilight of Sovereignty: How the Information Revolution Is Transforming Our World.* New York: S & S Trade, 1992.

Wu, Xindong. *Knowledge Acquisition from Databases.* Norwood, NJ: Ablex Publishing Co., 1995.

Wylie, Janet C. *Chances & Choices: How Women Can Succeed in Today's Knowledge Business.* Vienna, VA: EBW Press, 1996.

Zack, Michael H. *Knowledge and Strategy.* Woburn, MA: Butterworth-Heinemann, 1999.

Zuboff, Shoshana. *In the Age of the Smart Machine: The Future of Work and Power.* New York: Basic Books, 1989.

Zucker, Lynne G. *Intellectual Capital and the Birth of U.S. Biotechnology Enterprises.* Cambridge, MA: National Bureau of Economic Research, 1994.

Zucker, Lynne G. *Intellectual Capital and the Firm: The Technology of Geographically Localized Knowledge Spillovers.* Cambridge, MA: National Bureau of Economic Research, 1994.

ARTICLES

Due to the number of articles in this bibliography, the articles have been separated into subheadings (see Table of Contents). I hope that these more specialized divisions will assist the reader in locating and using the information contained herein.

KNOWLEDGE MANAGEMENT/BACKGROUND AND DEVELOPMENT

This group of articles serves very well as an introduction to the field of Knowledge Management. These articles tend to be broader in scope, thus providing a firm foundation upon which the reader can build. Knowledge Management is a relatively new field that is evolving and progressing rapidly. The concept of managing and utilizing data and information has existed for quite a while, but it was not until recently that its characteristics and identity came to be defined as a separate discipline. As the natural progression occurred, this field then matured into Knowledge Management, the next logical step. From compiling, processing and storing data to organizing the data (the creation of Information), and investing information with context and value beyond the information itself (the creation of Knowledge) to provide added value to the organization—whether it is in the for-profit or non-profit arena, or the private or public sectors.

As Knowledge Management found and developed its own niche, it continued to evolve and grow. Shortly thereafter, the niche became a functional entity, and the entity grew until it became a multi-faceted discipline. After all of these changes, Knowledge Management still continues to evolve. Continual evolution is the sign that, unlike other schools of thought in the management arena, Knowledge Management is not only here to stay but it will also continue its evolution into areas not yet imagined as more and more minds focus on it, add value to it, and take it further and further.

If one stops to think about it, Knowledge Management is the next logical, productive, and professional step in the way to conduct "business" whether or not the institution is a for-profit organization. Management experts have been talking for years about streamlining operations, increasing productivity, and creating revenue. Yet, until the advent of Knowledge Management, virtually every institution has not been applying the one ingredient it seeks in every employee—experience (Tacit Knowledge) to its every day pursuits.

More than many "management concepts," Knowledge Management is one concept that is useful, indeed necessary, outside of the working environment as well as within professional situations. In fact, most individuals who are at the top of their profession (whether it is in library science, the physical sciences, or any other discipline) have been practicing Knowledge Management before it had a name. They were seeking out and adding information to their skill set to enhance the value of their performance. Now that Knowledge Management has been identified and incorporated into many professional systems, these same individuals are now at the forefront in the application of Knowledge Management in their respective professions.

Knowledge Management, as stated above, has come to affect every field of human endeavor that deals with the collection, storage, dissemination, and synthesis of knowledge. The articles in this section discuss the beginnings and subsequent evolution of the subject as it has progressed from a concept to a philosophy to a working model.

Abell, Angela and Nigel Oxbrow. "Knowledge as a Corporate Resource: Moving Information to Center Stage." *IntraNet Professional* 01.01 (May 1998): 01, 07-08.

Alic, J. A. "Knowledge, Skill, and Education in the New Global Economy." *Futures* 29.01 (1997): 05-16.

Allee, Verna. "12 Principles of Knowledge Management." *Training & Development* 51.11 (November 1997): 71-74.

Allee, Verna. "Are You Getting Big Value from Knowledge?" *KMWorld* 08.09 (September 1999): 16-17.

Alter, Allan E. "Knowledge Management's 'Theory-Doing Gap'." *Computerworld* 34.15 (10 April 2000): 33.

Amidon, Debra M. "The Momentum of Knowledge Management." http://www. skyrme.com/entovatn/momentum.htm

Anderson, Gary. "A Needle in a Haystack." *Industry Week* 243.13 (04 July 1994): 41.

Angus, Jeff. "For Some, a Solid Knowledge-Management Foundation." *InformationWeek* 777 (13 March 2000): 94-95.

Anonymous. "Five Steps to Better Knowledge Management." *Computerworld* 29.25 (19 June 1995): ss03.

Arora, A. "Contracting for Tacit Knowledge: The Provision of Technical Services in Technology Licensing Contracts." *Journal of Developmental Economics* 50 (1996): 233-256.

Arthur, W. B. "Increasing Returns and the New World of Business." *Harvard Business Review* 74.04 (July-August 1998): 100-109.

Bajaria, H. J. "Knowledge Creation and Management: Inseparable Twins." *Total Quality Management* 11.04 (July 2000): 562-573.

Banks, H. "The Productivity Paradox." *Forbes* 144.02: 15.

Bartholomew, Doug. "Getting on Track: Alignment of Information Systems with Business Strategy Isn't Easy to Achieve or Maintain." *Industry Week* 247.05 (02 March 1998): 22-24.

Becerra-Fernandez, I. "Center for Innovation and Knowledge Management." *SIGGROUP Bulletin* 19.01: 46-51.

"Becoming Knowledge-Powered: Planning the Transformation." *Information Resources Management Journal* 13.01 (January-March 2000): 54-61.

Birkett, Bill. "Knowledge Management." *Chartered Accountants Journal of New Zealand* 74.01 (February 1995): 14-18.

Birkett, W. P. "Management Accounting and Knowledge Management." *Management Accounting* 77.05 (November 1995): 44-48.

Blair, David C. "The Management of Information: Basic Distinctions." *Sloan Management Review* 20.01 (Fall 1984): 13-23.

Blake, Paul. "The Future of Knowledge Management." *Information Today* 17.03 (March 2000): 14.

Blake, Paul. "The Knowledge Management Expansion." *Information Today* 15.01 (January 1998): 12-14.

Bogdan, Theresa A. "Knowledge Management." http://shrike.depaul.edu/%7 Etbogdan/ km.html

Bontis, Nick et al. "The Knowledge Toolbox: A Review of the Tools Available to Measure and Manage Intangible Resources." *European Management Journal* 17.04 (August 1999): 391-402.

Boyd, Stowe. "Knowledge Management in Context." *KMWorld* 08.08 (August 1999): 20, 25.

Brady, Roberta. "@BRINT—A Business Researcher's Interests." *Online* 22.05 (September-October 1998): 87.

Brandolese, A. and R. Cigolini. "A New Model for the Strategic Management of Inventories Subject to Peaks in Market Demand." *International Journal of Production Research* 37.08 (1999).

Bresnick, Peggy. "The Virtual Roundtable." *Insurance and Technology* 23.06 (June 1998): 76.

Brethenoux, E. "Knowledge Management: Myths and Challenges." *Gartner Group Research Note/Key Issues K-KMGT-1650* (1997).

Bruss, Lois R. "Ten Steps to Achieve KM Success." *KMWorld* 08.04 (April 1999): 37.

Butcher, David and Jennifer Rowley. "The 7 R's of Information Management." http://www.aslib.co.uk/man-inf/mar98/article1.html

"CAM-i Focuses on Knowledge Management." *Management-Accounting* 79 (November 1997): 66-67.

"Confusing Terminology." *Computerworld* (10 January 2000): 68.

Coombs, Rod and Richard Hall. "Knowledge Management Practices and Path-Dependency in Innovation." *Research Policy* 27.03 (July 1998): 237-253.

Cottrill, Ken. "Networking for Innovation." *Chemical Week* 160 (25 February 1998): 39-43.

Dataware Technologies, Inc. "Corporate Executive Briefing Linking People to Knowledge for Bottom Line Results." http://www.dataware.dk/kmswhite.htm

Davenport, Thomas H. "Some Principles of Knowledge Management." http://www.bus.utexas.edu/kman/kmprin.html

Davenport, Thomas H. and D. A. Marchand. "Is KM Just Good Information Management?" *The Financial Times* (08 March 1999): 02.

Davenport, Thomas H. and David E. Smith. "Managing Knowledge in Professional Service Firms." *Knowledge Directions* 01 (Spring 1999).

Davenport, Tom. "From Data to Knowledge." *CIO* (01 April 1999): 01-05.

"Defining Knowledge Management." *Public Relations Strategist* 04.02 (Summer 1998): 34-35.

"Delivering Knowledge into Your Hands." *Information Outlook* 03.06 (June 1999): 42-46.

Demarest, Marc. "Understanding Knowledge Management." *Long Range Planning* 30.03 (June 1997): 374-384.

Deveau, Denise. "Knowledge Is Business Power." *Computing Canada* 26.08 (14 April 2000): 14.

Dodge, John. "Will the Real Knowledge Management Please Stand Up?" *PC Week* 16.05 (01 February 1999): 03.

Dove, Rick. "A Knowledge Management Framework." *Automotive Manufacturing and Production* 110.01 (January 1998): 18-20.

Dragoon, A. "Knowledge Management: Rx for Success." *CIO* 08.18 (July 1995): 48-56.

Drucker, Peter F. "Beyond the Information Revolution." *The Atlantic Monthly* 284.04 (October 1999): 47-57.

Drucker, Peter F. "The Coming of the New Organization." *Harvard Business Review* 66.01 (January-February 1988): 45-53.

Drucker, Peter F. "The Information Executives Truly Need." *Harvard Business Review* (January-February 1995): 54.

Drucker, Peter F. "The Next Information Revolution." *Forbes ASAP* (24 August 1998): 47-58.

Duffy, Jan. "The KM Technology Infrastructure." *Information Management Journal* 34.02 (April 2000): 62-66.

Duhon, Bryant. "It's All in Our Heads." *Inform* 12.08 (September 1998): 09-13.

Dykeman, John B. "Knowledge Management Moves from Theory Toward Practice." *Managing Office Technology* 43.04 (May 1998): 12-14.

Dzinkowski, Ramona. "The Measurement and Management of Intellectual Capital: An Introduction." *Management Accounting* 78.02 (February 2000): 32-36.

Edwards, Ray. "Knowledge Management—A Culture, Not a Widget." *KMWorld* 06.16 (03 November 1997): 27, 39.

Emery, Priscilla. "Knowledge Management." *Inform* 11.10 (November 1997): 02.

"Fad Busters." *PC Week* 13.45 (11 November 1996): E03.

Fall, Andrew and Guy Mineau. "Knowledge Retrieval, Use and Storage for Efficiency." *Computational Intelligence* 15.01 (1999): 01.

Field, J. J. "Knowledge Management: A New Competitive Asset." *Information Outlook* 02.09: 27-30.

Finneran, Tom. "A Component-Based Knowledge Management System." http://www.tdan.com/i009hy04.htm

Fischbein, E. "Tacit Models." Tirosh, D., ed. *Implicit and Explicit Knowledge: An Educational Approach.* Norwood, NJ: Ablex Publishing Corp., 1994.

Fontaine, Michael. "Knowledge & Communities: An Annotated Bibliography 1991-1999." IBM Institute for Knowledge Management, August 1999.

Frappaolo, Carl. "Defining Knowledge Management: Four Basic Functions." *Computerworld* 32 (23 February 1998): 80.

Frappaolo, Carl. "Document Management's Role in Knowledge Management." *KMWorld* 07.10 (01 September 1998): 14, 16, 18.

Frappaolo, Carl and Wayne Toms. "Knowledge Management: From Terra Incognito to Terra Firma." *KMWorld* 06.15 (20 October 1997): 16-21.

Fryer, Bronwyn. "Get Smart." *Inc.* 21.13 (14 September 1999): 60-70.

Fuld, Leonard M. "Knowledge Profiteering." *CIO* 11.17 (15 June 1998): 28-32.

Fusaro, Roberta. "Knowledge Management Rescues Text Flood." *Computerworld* (11 January 1999): 74.

Gable, Guy G. "The Expert's Opinion." *Journal of Global Information Management* 08.02 (April-June 2000): 58-60.

Galagan, Patricia A. "Smart Companies." *Training & Development* 51.12 (December 1997): 20-24.

Gantz, John. "Knowledge Management: Some 'There' There." *Computerworld* 32.41 (12 October 1998): 33.

Gopal, Christopher and Joseph Gagnon. "Knowledge, Information, Learning and the IS Manager." *Computerworld* 29.25 (19 June 1995): ss01-ss07.

Gore, C. and E. Gore. "Knowledge Management: The Way Forward." *Total Quality Management* 10.04 (1999): S554-S560.

Grant, E. B. and J. J. Gregory. "Tacit Knowledge: The Life-Cycle and International Manufacturing Transfer." *Technology Analysis & Strategic Management* 09.02 (1997): 159-161.

Grayson, C. Jackson, Jr. and Carla S. O'Dell. "Mining Your Hidden Resources." *Across the Board* 35.04 (April 1998): 23-28.

Greengard, Samuel. "Storing, Shaping and Sharing Collective Wisdom." *Workforce* 77.10 (October 1998): 82-87.

Hannabuss, Stuart. "Knowledge Management." *Library Management* 08.05 (1987): 01-50.

Hansen, Morten T. et al. "What's Your Strategy for Managing Knowledge?" *Harvard Business Review* 77.02 (March-April 1999): 106-116.

Harari, Oren. "The Concrete Intangibles." *Management Review* 88.05 (May 1999): 30-33.

Harrington, Ann. "The Big Ideas: Ever Since Frederick Taylor Pulled out His Stopwatch, Big Thinkers Have Been Coming up with New—though Not Always Better—Ways to Manage People and Business. *Fortune* 140.10 (22 November 1999): 152+.

Helfer, Joe. "Order Out of Chaos: A Practitioner's Guide to Knowledge Management." *Searcher: The Magazine for Database Professionals* 06.07 (July-August 1998): 44-51.

Herbert, Ian. "Knowledge Is a Noun, Learning Is a Verb." *Management Accounting* 78.02 (February 2000): 68-69.

Hermans, John A. "Catch the Knowledge Management Wave." *Library Journal* 124.14 (01 September 1999): 161-163.

Hibbard, Justin. "Knowing What We Know." *InformationWeek* (20 October 1997): 46-64.

Holland, J. "Learning about Knowledge Management—CEST's Approach." *Assignation* 16.01 (October 1998): 05-09.

Houlder, Vanessa. "The High Price of Know-How." *The Financial Times* (14 July 1997): 10-11.

Israel, David and John Perry. "What Is Information?" http://www-csli.stanford.edu/~john/israel/whatisinfo/whatisinfo.html

Infield, Neil. "Capitalising on Knowledge." *Information World Review* 130 (November 1997): 22.

Inkpen, Andrew C. "Creating Knowledge through Collaboration." *California Management Review* 39.01 (Fall 1996): 123-140.

Jansen, M. G. and P. Beys. "On the Use of Meaningful Names in Knowledge-Based Systems." *Lecture Notes in Computer Science* (1999): 341-348.

Kalish, Doug. "EKM Traverses the Organization and Transcends Departmental Boundaries." *KMWorld* 08.09 (September 1999): 23-25, 37.

Kanter, Jerry. "Knowledge Management, Practically Speaking." *Information Systems Management* 16.04 (Fall 1999): 07-15.

Kepczyk, Roman H. "Knowledge Management Critical to Firm Futures." *Accounting Today* 14.04 (21 February 2000): 22.

"Knowledge Management: A Basic Q & A." *Information Advisor Knowledge Management Supplement* 01.01 (March 1997).

"Knowledge Management and Competitive Advantage." http://www.geo cities.com/Athens/Parthenon/5760/report.html

"Knowledge Management Consulting Gives CPAs a Competitive Edge." *CPA Journal* 68.08 (August 1998): 72.

"Knowledge Management: It's All About People." *Information Advisor* 11.06 (June 1999): 01.

"Knowledge Management: Managing Intellectual Capital Within an Organization." *PC Week* 14.35 (18 August 1997): 87.

Koenig, M. E. D. "A Bibliometric Analysis of Pharmaceutical Research." *Research Policy* 12.01: 15-36.

Koenig, M. E. D. "Bibliometric Indicators Versus Expert Judgement in Assessing Research Performance." *Journal of the American Society for Information Science* 43.02: 136-145.

Koenig, Michael E. D. "Education for Knowledge Management." *Information Services and Use* 19.01 (1999): 17.

Koenig, M. E. D. "Entering Stage III–The Convergence of the Stage Hypotheses." *Journal of the American Society for Information Science* 43.03: 204-207.

Koenig, Michael E. D. "Information Services and Productivity: A Background." Srikantaiah, Kanti and Michael E. D. Koenig, eds. *Knowledge Management for the Information Professional.* Medford, NJ: Information Today, 1999.

Koenig, Michael E. D. and T. Kanti Srikantaiah. "The Evolution of Knowledge Management." Srikantaiah, Kanti and Michael E. D. Koenig, eds. *Knowledge*

Management for the Information Professional. Medford, NJ: Information Today, 1999.

Koulopolos, Thomas. "Knowledge Management: Toward Creating the 'Knowing Enterprise'." *KMWorld* 07.02 (23 February 1998).

Kramer, Matt. "Knowledge Management Becomes Catch Phrase But Eludes Easy Definition." *PC Week* (07 December 1998): 95.

Lettis, Lucy. "When Less Is More." *Information Outlook* 02.05 (May 1998): 17-20.

Licklider, J. C. R. "Man-Computer Symbiosis." www. memex.org/licklider.pdf

Lim, K. K. et al. "Managing for Quality through Knowledge Management." *Total Quality Management* 65.07 (1999): S615-S621.

Lindsey-King, C. "Knowledge Management: Your Link to the Future." *Bibliotheca Medica Canadiana* 20.02 (Winter 1998): 74-75.

Lloyd, Bruce. "Knowledge Management: The Key to Long-Term Organizational Success." *Long Range Planning* 29.04 (August 1996): 576-580.

Lloyd, Bruce. "The Wisdom of the World: Messages for the New Millennium." *The Futurist* 34.03 (May 2000): 42.

Macintosh, Ann. "Position Paper on Knowledge Asset Management." http://www. aiai.ed.ac.uk/~alm/kam.html

Maglitta, Joseph. "Know-How, Inc." *Computerworld* 30.01 (15 January 1996): 73-75.

Maglitta, Joseph. "Smarten Up!" *Computerworld* 29.23 (05 June 1995): 84-86.

"Making Aid Work." *The Economist* 349.8094: 88.

Malhotra, Yogesh. "From Information Management to Knowledge Management: Beyond the 'Hi-Tech Hidebound' Systems." Srikantaiah, Kanti and M. E. D. Koenig, eds. *Knowledge Management for the Information Professional.* Medford, NJ: Information Today, 1999.

Malhotra, Yogesh. "Knowledge Management and New Organization Forms: A Framework for Business Model Innovation." *Information Resources Management Journal* 13.01 (January-March 2000): 05-14.

Malhotra, Yogesh. "Knowledge Management for the New World of Business." http://www.brint.com

Malhotra, Yogesh. "Managing the Business of Knowledge in Interesting Times." *Information Resources Management Journal* 13.01 (January-March 2000): 03-04.

Management Review. "Survey on Knowledge Management." *Management Review* 88.04 (April 1999): 20-23.

Mannes, Suzanne and Shelli M. Hoyes. "Reinstating Knowledge during Reading: A Strategic Process." *Discourse Processes* 21.01 (January-February 1996): 105-130.

Manville, B. and N. Foote. "Harvest Your Workers' Knowledge." *Datamation* 42.13 (July 1996): 78-80.

Marchand, Donald A. "Information Management: Strategies and Tools in Transition?" *Information Management Review* 01.01 (1985): 27-34.

"Marks & Spencer." *Windows on Retail & Distribution* 07.15: 17-18.

"Mastering Information Management." *The Financial Times* (08 March 1999): 01-15.

Mayo, Andrew. "Memory Bankers." *People Management* 04 (22 January 1998): 34-38.

Mazzie, Mark. "Key Challenges Facing the Evolution of Knowledge Management." Srikantaiah, Kanti and Michael E. D. Koenig, eds. *Knowledge Management for the Information Professional.* Medford, NJ: Information Today, 1999.

McKinley, Tony. "A First Step Toward Knowledge Management." *KMWorld* 07.09 (01 August 1998): 36-37.

McKinley, Tony. "What Is KM All About?" *KMWorld* 07.02 (23 February 1998): 01, 25, 39.

McLean, Neil. "Challenges in the Information Services Market." *Australian Library Journal* 46.01 (February 1997): 52-67.

McWilliams, Gary and Marcia Stepanek. "Knowledge Management: Taming the Info Monster." *Business Week* 3583 (22 June 1998): 170-172.

Meyer, Christopher. "What Makes Workers Tick?" *Inc.* 19 (December 1997): 74-75.

Middleton, M. "From Information Management to Knowledge Management: Some Perspectives on Development." *El Profesional de la Informacion* 08.05 10-17.

Milne, J. "Think Tank." *Unix & NT News* 129 (December 1999-January 2000): 18-20.

"Mr. Knowledge." *The Economist* (31 May 1997): 63.

Mueller, Nancy S. "Missing the Competitive-Advantage Boat." *Managing Office Technology* 42.01 (January 1997): 22.

Mullins, Craig. "What Is Knowledge and Can It Be Managed?" http://www.tdan.com/i008fe03.htm

Murray, Philip. "New Language for New Leverage: The Terminology of Knowledge Management." http://www.ktic.com

"Navigating Among the Disciplines: The Library and Interdisciplinary Inquiry." *Library Trends* 45.02 (Fall 1996).

Newman, Brian. "Knowledge Management vs. Knowledge Engineering." http://revolution.3-cities.com

O'Leary, D. E. "Enterprise Knowledge Management." *Computer* 31.03 (March 1998): 54-61.

Oliver, Amalya L. and Kathleen Montgomery. "Creating a Hybrid Organizational Form from Parental Blueprints: The Emergence and Evolution of Knowledge Firms." *Human Relations* 53.01 (January 2000): 33-56.

Owen, T. "Knowledge Management: What We Need to Do to Stay in the Swim." *Assignation* 16.01 (October 1998): 19-21.

Oxbrow, N. and A. Abell. "Knowledge Management: Competitive Advantage for the 21st Century." *Records Management Bulletin* 83 (December 1997): 05-10.

Pascarella, Perry. "Harnessing Knowledge." *Management Review* 86.09 (October 1997): 37-40.

Pastore, Richard. "The Importance of Getting Smart." *CIO* 08.11 (15 March 1995): 62-66.

Pemberton, J. Michael. "Knowledge Management (KM) and the Epistemic Tradition." *Records Management Quarterly* 32.03 (July 1998): 58-62.

Penttila, Chris. "Who Knows?" *Entrepreneur* 28.04 (April 2000): 138-141.

Pinelli, Thomas E. and Rebecca O. Barclay. "Maximizing the Results of Federally-Funded Research and Development Through Knowledge Management: A Strategic Imperative for Improving U.S. Competitiveness." *Government Information Quarterly* 15.02 (1998): 157-172.

Ponelis, S. and F. A. Fairer-Wessels. "Knowledge Management: A Literature Overview." *South African Journal of Library and Information Science* 66.01 (March 1998): 01-09.

Prusak, Larry. "Where Did Knowledge Management Come From?" *Knowledge Directions* 01 (Fall 1999): 90-96.

Riley, Bryan. "You Are Now Entering the Age of the Mind: Thoughts on the Knowledge Society." *Australian Library Journal* 47.02 (May 1998): 145-156.

Roberts-Witt, Sarah L. "Knowledge Management: Know What You Know." *PC Magazine* (01 July 2000): 165.

Rogers, Debra M. "Knowledge Management Gains Momentum in Industry." *Research-Technology Management* 39.03 (May-June 1996): 05-07.

Ross, Cynthia. "IT 'Craze': Management of Knowledge New IT 'Craze'." *Computing Canada* (13 July 1998).

Rowland, Hillary. "Doctor Know." *People Management* 04.05 (05 March 1998): 50-52.

Saffady, William. "Digital Library Concepts and Technologies for the Management of Library Collections: An Analysis of Methods and Costs." *Library Technology Reports* 31.03 (May-June 1995): 221-379.

Schmalhofer, F. and L. Van Elst. "An Oligo-Agents System with Shared Responsibilities for Knowledge Management." *Lecture Notes in Computer Science* 1621 (1999): 379-384.

Schmidt, David P. "Ethics for Knowledge Management." Srikantaiah, Kanti and Michael E. D. Koenig, eds. *Knowledge Management for the Information Professional.* Medford, NJ: Information Today, 1999.

Schrage, Michael. "John Seely Brown." *Wired* 08.08 (August 2000): 204-207.

Schrage, Michael. "Why Stop at Knowledge Management?" *Computerworld* 30.46 (11 November 1996): 37.

Sherwell, J. "Building the Virtual Library: The Case of SmithKline Beecham." *Managing Information* 04.05 35-36.

Shockley, William III. "Planning for Knowledge Management." *Quality Progress* 33.03 (March 2000).

Silver, Bruce. "Everything You Really Need to Know about KM." *KMWorld* 07.13 (December 1998): 20.

Skyrme, David J. "Knowledge Management: Oxymoron or Dynamic Duo?" *Managing Information* 04.07 (September 1997): 24-26.

Smith, Geoff. "The Journey of a Thousand Miles Starts with a Single Step." *Knowledge Management* (December 1999-January 2000): 24-25.

Smith, Keith. "Managing Knowledge." *Supply Management* 40.02 (27 January 2000).

Smith, Rebecca A. "Knowledge: Researching the Power Base of the Organization." *Information Outlook* 02.06 (June 1998): 12-14.

Songini, Marc. "Knowledge Management a Murky Subject." (05 October 1999). http://features.idg.net/crd_knowledge_87092.html

"Special Focus: Knowledge Management." *Journal of Business Strategy* 19 (January-February 1998): 10-28.

"Special Issue: Knowledge Management." *Harvard Business Review* 74 (July-August 1997).

"Special Issue: Knowledge Management." *Harvard Business Review* 75 (September-October 1997).

Spender, J. "Competitive Advantage from Tacit Knowledge? Unpacking the Concept and Its Strategic Implications." Moingeon, Bertrand and Amy

Edmondson, eds., *Organizational Learning and Competitive Advantage.* Thousand Oaks, CA: Sage Publications, 1996.

Srikantaiah, T. Kanti. "An Introduction to Knowledge Management." Srikantaiah, Kanti and Michael E. D. Koenig, eds. *Knowledge Management for the Information Professional.* Medford, NJ: Information Today, 1999.

Srikantaiah, T. Kanti. "Knowledge Management: A Faceted Overview." Srikantaiah, Kanti and Michael E. D. Koenig, eds. *Knowledge Management for the Information Professional.* Medford, NJ: Information Today, 1999.

Sternberg, R. J. et al. "Practical Intelligence: The Nature and Role of Tacit Knowledge in Work and at School." Puckett, J. M. and H. W. Reese, eds. *Mechanisms of Everyday Cognition.* Hillsdale, NJ: Lawrence Erlbaum Associates.

Stewart, Thomas A. "Taking Risk to the Marketplace." *Fortune* 141.05 (06 March 2000): 424. IC.

Streatfield, David and Tom Wilson. "Deconstructing 'Knowledge Management'." *ASLIB Proceedings* 51.03 (March 1999): 67-71.

Stuart, Ann. "Five Uneasy Pieces, Part Two: Knowledge Management." *CIO* (01 June 1997).

Stuller, Jay. "Chief of Corporate Smarts." *Training* 35.04 (April 1998): 28-34.

Tan, Jeffrey. "Knowledge Management—Just More Buzzwords?" *British Journal of Administrative Management* 19.10 (March-April 2000): 10.

"Tapping Corporate Knowledge." *Internal Auditor* 55.04 (August 1998): 15-16.

Tebbe, Mark. "No, Those Aren't Documents; They're 'Knowledge Sources'." *InfoWorld* 21.16 (19 April 1999): 30.

"Think Leadership Articles." http://www.ibm.com/thinkmag/articles/pplpower/pplpower.html

"Tips for Know-How." *Computerworld* 32.04 (26 January 1998): s06.

"Tips for Making Knowledge Management Pay Off." *IT Cost Management Strategies* 16.04 (April 1997): 07-08.

Trussler, Simon. "The Rules of the Game." *Journal of Business Strategy* 19 (January-February 1998): 16-19.

Vollmer, Mike and Tessy Phillips. "Process Mapping Key Starter in Knowledge Management." *Offshore* 60.04 (April 2000): 130-131.

Wagner, R. K. and R. J. Sternberg. "Practical Intelligence in Real-World Pursuits: The Role of Tacit Knowledge." *Journal of Personality and Social Psychology* 49.02 (1985): 436-458.

Wah, Louisa. "Behind the Buzz." *Management Review* 88.04 (April 1999): 16-26.

Waldron, M. "Mental Wealth." *Document Manager* 08.01 (January-February 2000): 36-39.

Watson, Sharon. "Getting to 'Aha!'." *Computerworld* 32.04 (26 January 1998): s01-s05.

Wetteland, Annette, ed. "Iowa: Making the Information Connection." *Library Hi Tech* 14.02-03 (1996): 115-123.

"What Is Knowledge Management (KM)?" http://www.sims.berkeley.edu/courses/is213/s99/Projects/P9/web_site/about_km.html

Whiting, Rick. "Myths & Realities." *Informationweek* 762 (22 November 1999): 42-54.

Wiig, Karl M. "On the Management of Knowledge." http://revolution.3-cities.com/~bonewman/wiig.htm

Wiig, K. M. "Knowledge Management: Where Did It Come From and Where Will It Go?" *Expert Systems with Applications* 13.01 (July 1997): 01-14.

Wiig, K. M. et al. "Supporting Knowledge Management: A Selection of Methods and Techniques." *Expert Systems with Applications* 13.01 (July 1997): 15-27.

Winter, Michael F. "Specialization, Territoriality, and Jurisdiction: Librarianship and the Political Economy of Knowledge." *Library Trends* 45.02 (Fall 1996): 343-363.

Wolff, M. F. "Knowledge Management Gains Momentum in Industry." *Research Technology Management* 39.03 (May 1996): 05-07.

Young, Ron. "The Wide-Awake Club." *People Management* 04 (05 February 1998): 46-49.

Yu, Dorothy. "Managing Knowledge Correctly Can Transform High-Tech." *Boston Business Journal* 20.01 (11 February 2000): 09-10.

INTELLECTUAL CAPITAL

What is an asset? According to the *New Shorter Oxford English Dictionary*, it is "a thing or person of use or value." If one asks an accountant for examples of assets, one will get an array of answers: accounts receivable, bonds, buildings, cash, certificates of deposit, equipment, "goodwill," land, physical plant, stocks…the list goes on and on. Several years ago, if one were to ask an accountant the value of a firm's Intellectual Capital—one would most likely have been greeted with a blank look, and a hurried excuse to go to an "imaginary" meeting. Now Intellectual Capital is sought as eagerly and intensely as profit. Why? Because Intellectual Capital has and has had a constant and significant impact on profit whether or not it was measured. Greater effectiveness, greater efficiency, greater employee involvement, higher employee morale, and increased productivity are among the results that properly managed Intellectual Capital can produce. Explicit and Tacit Knowledge are what make the business world go round. The value of Explicit Knowledge has long been known, but the greater value of Tacit Knowledge is finally being addressed. If Tacit Knowledge cannot be located, collected, stored, and distributed in a timely manner to those who need and can use it, then a firm will not last very long.

The value of Intellectual Capital has been quantified. It is valuable in the corporate suite, it is valuable to the Administrative Assistant, it is valuable in the hallowed halls of academia, and it is also has value on the floor of a factory. Ask any productive employee at any level: Who does one call to ensure that an "emergency" task gets done correctly and on time the first time? That information is worth its weight in gold to any organization. Every employee knows the answer to that question after a period of time, but wouldn't it be better if every employee knew the answer as soon as it was needed? This type of knowledge has been around since the beginning of the business world and its value is in direct proportion to the effort and time required to locate the answer.

Knowledge of one's given field has always been a requirement for an individual to perform productively in a professional environment. Given the explosion of inter-disciplinary functions and operations, it is now essential that if one does not have expertise in another, separate discipline, then one needs to know where the requisite expertise lies and how to get access to it in a timely manner. It is only recently that various forms of endeavor have identified Intellectual Capital as an asset that not only needs to be defined and utilized, but also valued and pursued as much as a positive cash flow.

This section discusses the collection, compilation, storage, accessibility, and utilization of this long-overlooked but indispensable asset.

"Abuzz' Beehive Selected by Customers Including Micro Modeling, American Management Systems to Manage People-Based Intellectual Capital." *PR Newswire* 5891 (10 May 1999).

Agor, Weston H. "The Measurement, Use, and Development of Intellectual Capital to Increase Public Sector Productivity." *Public Personnel Management* 26.02 (Summer 1997): 175-186.

Alter, Allan E. "Is Knowledge Management in Trouble?" *Computerworld* 32.24 (15 June 1998): 75.

Aoki, R. and T. J. Prusa. "International Standards for Intellectual Property Protection and R & D Incentives." *Journal of International Economics* 35.02 (1993): 251-273.

Barchan, Margetta. "Capturing Knowledge for Business Growth." *Knowledge Management Review* 04 (September-October 1998): 12-15.

Barsky, Noah P. and Garry Marchant. "The Most Valuable Resource— Measuring and Managing Intellectual Capital." *Strategic Finance* (February 2000): 58-62.

Bassi, Laurie J. "Harnessing the Power of Intellectual Capital." *Training & Development* 51.12 (December 1997): 25-30.

Bassi, Laurie J. and Brian Hackett. "Leveraging Intellectual Capital." *HR Executive Review* 05.03.

Bell, Chip R. "Intellectual Capital." *Executive Excellence* 14 (January 1999): 15-17.

Bender, David R. "It's the Way You Use It." *Information Outlook* 02.10 (October 1998): 05.

Berry, John. "Real Knowledge Is Held by People." *InternetWeek* (10 January 2000): 31.

Bolita, Dan. "Intellectual Assets—A Price on (What's in) Your Head." *KMWorld* 08.02 (February 1999): 24, 27.

Bontis, Nick. "Intellectual Capital: An Exploratory Study that Develops Measures and Models." *Management Decision* 36.02 (1998): 63-76.

Bontis, Nick. "Managing Organizational Knowledge by Diagnosing Intellectual Capital: Framing and Advancing the State of the Field." *International Journal of Technology Management* 18.05-08 (1999): 433-462.

Bontis, Nick. "There's a Price on Your Head: Managing Intellectual Capital Strategically." *Business Quarterly* 60.04 (Summer 1996): 40-47.

Bowes, R. "How Best to Find and Fulfill Business Information Needs." *ASLIB Proceedings* 47.05 (May 1995): 119-126.

Bradley, Keith. "Intellectual Capital and the New Wealth of Nations." *Business Strategy Review* 08.01 (Spring 1997): 53-62.

Bradley, Keith. "Intellectual Capital and the New Wealth of Nations II." *Business Strategy Review* 08.04 (Winter 1997): 33-44.

Brenner, Pamela M. "Knowledge Management. Motivating Knowledge Workers. The Role of the Workplace. Meeting Basic Needs Can Help Companies Attract and Retain Valuable Employees and Their Intellectual Capital." *Quality Progress* 32.01 (1999): 33.

Brooking, Annie. "Knowledge Management and Corporate Memory." *Intellectual Capital: Core Asset for the Third Millennium Enterprise.* London: International Thomson Business Press, 1996.

Brooking, Annie. "The Management of Intellectual Capital." *Long Range Planning* 30.03 (June 1997): 364-365.

Brown, Tom. "Ringing Up Intellectual Capital." *Management* 87.01 (January 1998): 47-50.

Bukowitz, Wendi R. and Gordon P. Petrash. "Visualizing, Measuring, and Managing Knowledge." *Research Technology Management* 40 (July-August 1997): 24-31.

Caron, Marie-Andree. "Adding Value." *CMA Management* 73.06 (July-August 1999): 35-37.

Caulkin, Simon. "The Knowledge Within." *Management Today* (August 1997): 28-32.

Cohen, Stephen L. and Nena K. Backer. "Making and Mining Intellectual Capital: Method or Madness?" *Training & Development* 53.09 (September 1999): 46-50.

Cole-Gomolski, Barb. "Knowledge Management Effort at Dow Helps Company Rein in Patents, Data." *ComputerWorld* 32 (05 January 1998): 49-53.

Comeau-Kirschner, Cheryl. "The Sharing Culture." *Management Review* (January 2000): 08.

Crainer, Stuart. "The Swedes Are Coming." *Across the Board* 36.06 (June 1999): 31-35.

Czerniawska, Fiona. "From Intellectual Capital to Intellectual Income." *Knowledge Management* (December 1999-January 2000): 32.

Dakers, H. "Intellectual Capital: Auditing the People Assets." *INSPEL* 32.04 (1998): 234-242.

Davies, Jan and Alan Waddington. "The Management and Measurement of Intellectual Capital." *Management Accounting-London* 77.08 (September 1999): 34.

Dearlove, Des. "From Brawn to Brainpower." *The Times* (08 May 1997): s04.

Deavenport, Earnie. "Intellectual Capital: The Key to Growing Shareowner Value." *Executive Speeches* 12 (February-March 1998): 01-03.

Donlon, J. P. "Knowledge Capital." *Chief Executive* 120 (January-February 1997): 52-61.

Donnelly, George. "It's the Intellectual Capital, Stupid!" *CFO, The Magazine for Senior Financial Executives* 15.04 (April 1999): 26.

Downes, Meredith and Anisya S. Thomas. "Knowledge Transfer through Expatriation: The U-Curve Approach to Overseas Staffing." *Journal of Managerial Issues* 12.02 (Summer 2000): 131-149.

Dzinkowski, Ramona. "Managing the Brain Trust." *CMA Management* 73.08 (October 1999): 14-18.

Dzinkowski, Ramona. "Mining Intellectual Capital." *Strategic Finance* 81.04 (October 1999): 42-46.

Edvinsson, Leif. "Developing Intellectual Capital at Skandia." *Long Range Planning* 30.03 (June 1997): 366-373.

Edvinsson, Leif. "Visualizing Intellectual Capital in Skandia." *Skandia's 1994 Annual Report.* Stockholm, Sweden: Skandia AFS, 1995.

Edwards, Steven. "The Brain Gain." *CA Magazine* 130 (April 1997): 20-25.

Ellerbee, Linda. "CEO's Notebook—A Low-Tech, Low-Cost Way to Maximize the Intellectual Capital of Your Staff; The Benefits of On-the-Job Mapping; Targeted Surveys for Successful Concept Testing; Spotlight on the Rate of Small-Business Failure; and 'My Biggest Mistake'." *Inc.* 21.09 (1999): 79.

"Evaluating the Value of Knowledge Capital." *CPA Journal* 68.07 (July 1998): 57.

"Financial Reporting—Statement of Intellectual Capital." *Accountancy* 123.1266 (1999): 84.

"Forbes2000.com: The Killer App for 2000." http://www.intellectualcapital.com

"From the Back—Smart Cookies—Intellectual Capital: What's It Worth to You?" *Management Today* (April 1999): 97.

Gautschi, Ted. "Develop Your Intellectual Capital." *Design News* 53.14 (20 July 1998): 170.

Gautschi, Ted. "Does Your Firm Manage Knowledge?" *Design News* 54.11 (07 June 1999): 188.

Gautschi, Ted. "The Knowledge Continuum." *Design News* 54.12 (21 June 1999): 170.

Gautschi, Ted. "Managing Your Company's Intellectual Assets." *Design News* 54.18 (20 September 1999): 261.

Geisler, Eliezer. "Harnessing the Value of Experience in the Knowledge-Driven Firm." *Business Horizons* 42.03 (01 May 1999): 18.

Gill, Kathleen D. "Knowledge Management: Tapping, Directing, Intellectual Capital Helps Employees Share What They Know." *Human Resources Report* 15 (22 September 1997): 21-25.

Halliday, Leah. "Corporate Information: Stored but Not Retrieved." *Knowledge Management* (December 1999-January 2000): 33.

Hanauer, Joe. "Your Information: What It's Worth." *Today's Realtor* 31.07 (July 1998): 20-21.

"A Hands-On Look at Intellectual Capital." *Management Review* 87 (January 1998): 50-51.

Harvey, Michael G. and Robert F. Lusch. "Balancing the Intellectual Capital Books: Intangible Liabilities." *European Management Journal* (February 1999): 85-92.

Hermans, John A. "Managing Knowledge Workers: New Skills and Attitudes to Unlock the Intellectual Capital in Your Organization." *Library Journal* 124.14 (01 September 1999): 161-163.

Hickins, Michael. "Gray Matter Stolen." *Management Review* 88.08 (September 1999): 06.

Hoffman, Carl. "BIC Makes It Happen." *Appalachia: Journal of the Appalachian Regional Commission* 32.01 (01 January 1999): 24.

Horvath, Joseph A. "White Paper: Working with Tacit Knowledge." IBM Institute for Knowledge Management, April 1999.

"The Human Dimension." *Business Asia* 31.18 (06 September 1999): 02-04.

"Intellectual Capital." *Inc.* 60 (15 September 1999).

"Investing in Intellectual Capital." *Education & Training* 41.02 (1999): 150.

Jeffers, Michelle. "Here Come the Consultants: Corporate America Soon Will Spend Billions on IC." *Forbes ASAP* 159.07 (07 April 1997): s70.

Kalisky, Lorin David. "Managing Knowledge: Turn Your Information into Valuable Gems." *Publish* 15.03 (March 2000): 75-76. IC.

Kennie, T. "Practice Direction: Is Knowledge and Intellectual Capital Management a Fashionable Fad?" *The New Law Journal* (1999): 893.

King, Alfred M. and Jay M. Henry. "Valuing Intangible Assets through Appraisals." *Strategic Finance* 81.05 (November 1999): 32-37.

Kinney, Thomas J. "Knowledge Management, Intellectual Capital and Adult Learning." *Adult Learning,* 10.02 (Winter 1998-1999): 02-03.

Kirtley, Robert et al. "Crossing the Threshold to the Age of Ideas." *KMWorld* 08.02 (February 1999): 26-27.

Knight, Daniel J. "Performance Measures for Increasing Intellectual Capital." *Strategy & Leadership* 27.02 (March-April 1999): 22-27.

Koenig, M. E. D. "The Convergence of Computers and Telecommunications, Information Management Implications." *Information Management Review* 01.03 (September 1986): 23-33.

Koenig, M. E. D. "From Intellectual Capital to Knowledge Management: What Are They Talking About?" *INSPEL* 32.04 (1998): 222-233.

Koenig, M. E. D. "Intellectual Capital and How to Leverage It." *Bottom Line* 10.03 (1997): 112-118.

Koenig, M. E. D. "Intellectual Capital and Knowledge Management." *IFLA Journal* 22.04 (1996): 299-301.

Kogut, Bruce. "The Network as Knowledge: Generative Rules and the Emergence of Structure." *Strategic Management Journal* 21.03 (March 2000): 405-425.

Kurtzman, Joel. "A Mind Is a Terrible Thing to Waste." *Chief Executive* 112 (April 1996): 20.

Leavitt, Wendy. "The Brains of the Outfit." *Fleet Owner* 94.08 (August 1999): 81.

Lenzner, Robert and Carrie Shook. "Whose Rolodex Is It, Anyway?" *Forbes* 161 (23 February 1998): 100-104.

Liebowitz, Jay and Ching Y. Suen. "Developing Knowledge Management Metrics for Measuring Intellectual Capital." *Journal of Intellectual Capital* 01.01 (14 April 2000): 54-67.

Little, Stephen. "Global Production and Global Consumption: Designing Organisations and Networks for the Next Century." *Creativity and Innovation Management* 08.01 (1999): 08.

Lockenhoff H. "Knowledge Management. Activating Intellectual Capital." *Knowledge Organization* 24.04 (1997): 255-258.

Longford, Ross. "Funding Intellectual Capital: The Valuation Dilemma." *Australian CPA* 69.07 (August 1999): 22-23.

Malhotra, Yogesh. "Knowledge Assets in the Global Economy: Assessment of National Intellectual Capital." *Journal of Global Information Management* 08.03 (July-September 2000): 05-15.

Markham, Lyndsay. "Tales from the New Economy." *Knowledge Management* (December 1999-January 2000): 12-17.

Masood, Ehsan. "...in the Push for a Knowledge-Driven Economy." *Nature* (18 March 1999): 181.

Mastorovich, Mary Jane. "Intellectual Capital: Participatory Models of Hospital Work Process Redesign." *MedSurg Nursing* 07.03 (1998): 172.

Mayo, Andrew. "Called to Account." *People Management* 05.07 (08 April 1999): 33.

McKinley, James M. "Planning for Success after 'Go-Live'." *Strategic Finance* 81.10 (April 2000): 54-58.

McRae, Hamish. "Small Firms Nurture Big Brains." *Director* 50.06 (January 1997): 64-65.

"Measuring Intellectual Assets." http://www.montague.com/le/le1096.html

"Measuring Training's Contribution to Intellectual Capital." *Training* 35 (March 1998): 14-16.

Messmer, Max. "Mentoring: Building Your Company's Intellectual Capital." *HR Focus* 75.09 (September 1998): S11-S12.

Miller, Marlane. "Leveraging Your Hardwired Intellectual Capital." *Strategy & Leadership* 27.02 (March-April 1999): 28-32.

Miller, William. "Building the Ultimate Resource." *Management Review* 88.01 (January 1999): 42-45.

Miller, William. "Features—Human Resources." *Management Review* 88.01 (1999): 41.

Miller, William C. "Fostering Intellectual Capital." *HR Focus* 75.01 (January 1998): 09-10.

Mintz, S. L. "A Knowing Glance." *CFO: The Magazine for Chief Financial Officers* 16.02 (February 2000): 52-54.

Mirabile, Rick. "Technology and Intellectual Capital: The New Revolution." *Human Resources Professional* 11.04 (July-August 1998): 19-22.

Moad, Jeff. "How to Know about Knowledge." *PC Week* 15.24 (15 June 1998): 128.

Molsbee, Allan. "Don't Overlook the Intangibles." *Manufacturing Engineering* 124.03 (March 2000): 232.

Nahapiet, Janine and Sumantra Ghoshal. "Social Capital, Intellectual Capital, and the Organizational Advantage." *The Academy of Management Review* 23.02 (April 1998): 242-266.

"News and Trends." *CA Magazine* 132.04 (01 May 1999): 12.

Oesterholm, J.-E. and V. Ukkola. "Stacking Up: Intellectual Capital Is Not Just About Patents and Trade Marks." *Managing Intellectual Property* 89 (1999): 30.

Parkes, Hugh. "Valuing Intelligence: Rethinking Some Fundamentals." *Australian Accountant* 67 (November 1997): 28-31.

Petty, Richard and James Guthrie. "Managing Intellectual Capital: From Theory to Practice." *Australian CPA* 69.07 (August 1999): 18-21.

Phillips, Tessy and Mike Vollmer. "Knowledge Management in the Current Marketplace." *Oil & Gas Journal* (Spring 2000): 04-05.

Rastogi, P. N. "Knowledge Management and Intellectual Capital: The New Virtuous Reality of Competitiveness." *Human Systems Management* 19.01 (2000): 39-48.

"Reengineering Corporate Training: Intellectual Capital and Transfer of Learning." *Journal of Career Planning & Employment* 59.02 (Winter 1999): 15-16.

Reid, Joanne. "Tom Stewart on Intellectual Capital." *Ivey Business Quarterly* 62.03 (Spring 1998): 15-18.

Roberts, Bill. "Pick Employees' Brains." *HR Magazine* (February 2000): 115-120.

Roos, Johan. "Exploring the Concept of Intellectual Capital." *Long Range Planning* 31.01 (February 1998): 150-153.

Roslender, Robin. "Accounting for Intellectual Capital: A Contemporary Management Accounting Perspective." *Management Accounting* 78.03 (March 2000): 34-37.

Sammers, Joanne. "Ideas in the Zone: Profitable Ideas Fuel Mercer's Advance." http://consultingcentral.com/features/nov1999profile.html

Scarbrough, Harry. "Knowledge as Work: Conflicts in the Management of Knowledge Workers." *Technology, Analysis and Strategic Management* 11.01 (1999): 05.

Schmitz, Ron. "Protecting Intellectual Capital by Managing Information." *Appliance Manufacturer* 47.10 (Octpber 1999): 84.

Shand, Dawne. "Why Do Intellectual Capital Measures Focus on the Wrong Subject?" *KMWorld* 08.02 (February 1999): 26.

"Skandia: The Pioneer of Intellectual Capital Reporting." *Business Strategy Review* 08.04 (Winter 1997): 38-41.

Smith, Rebecca A. "Knowledge: Researching the Power Base of the Organization." *Information Outlook* 02.06 (June 1998): 12-13.

"Special Issue: Intellectual Capital." *Forbes ASAP* (07 April 1997).

"Special Issue: Intellectual Capital." *Long Range Planning* (June 1997).

"Special Issue: The Epistemological Challenge: Managing Knowledge and Intellectual Capital." *European Management Journal* 14 (August 1996).

"Statement of Intellectual Capital." *Accountancy* (01 February 1999): 84.

Stewart, Thomas A. "Brainpower." *Fortune* 123.11 (03 June 1991): 44-51.

Stewart, Thomas A. "Getting Real about Brainpower." *Fortune* 132.11 (27 November 1995): 201-203.

Stewart, Thomas A. "Gray Flannel Suit? Moi?" *Fortune* 137 (16 March 1998): 76-82.

Stewart, Thomas A. "How a Little Company Won Big by Betting on Brainpower." *Fortune* 132.05 (04 September 4 1995): 121-122.

Stewart, Thomas A. "Now Capital Means Brains, Not Just Bucks." *Fortune* 123.01 (14 January 1991): 31-33.

Stewart, Thomas A. "Your Company's Most Valuable Asset: Intellectual Capital." *Fortune* 130.07 (03 October 1994): 68-73.

Stivers, Bonnie P. et al. "How Non-Financial Performance Measures Are Used." *Management Accounting* 79 (February 1998): 44-46.

Sveiby, Karl-Erik. "Intellectual Capital: Thinking Ahead." *Australian CPA* 68.05 (June 1998): 18-22.

Swanborg, Rick and Bob Reck. "Grow Your Own Consultants." *CIO* 12.13 (15 April 1999): 76-77.

Tapp, Lawrence G. "Management Education in Canada." *Ivey Business Quarterly* 62.03 (Spring 1998): 07-09.

Tapsell, Sherrill. "Making Money from Brainpower." *Management-Auckland* 45.06 (July 1998): 36-43.

Tynan, Susan A. "Best Behaviors." *Management Review* 88.10 (November 1999): 58-61.

Ulrich, Dave. "Intellectual Capital Equals Competence x Commitment." *Sloan Management Review* 39.02 (Winter 1998): 15-26.

Van Buren, Mark E. "A Yardstick for Knowledge Management." *Training & Development* 53.05 (May 1999): 71-77.

"A Viking with a Compass: Leif Edvinsson's Technique for Measuring Intellectual Capital." *The Economist* (06 June 1998): 64.

Weber, Pamela F. "Getting a Grip on Employee Growth." *Training & Development* 53.05 (May 1999): 87-92.

"When Intellectual Capital Starts Heading for the Door." *Management Today* (February 1999): 09-10.

Wiig, Karl M. "Integrating Intellectual Capital and Knowledge Management." *Long Range Planning* 30.03 (June 1997): 399-405.

Wileman, Andrew. "A Capital Idea." *Management Today* (April 1999): 97.

KNOWLEDGE MANAGEMENT AND THE LEARNING ORGANIZATION

Continuing education, continuation training, as well as seminar and conference attendance are prerequisites for any employee who wants to remain abreast of current events, innovations, and issues in his or her respective area of expertise. If the whole is equal to the sum of its parts, then the organization as a whole must move forward as well. The organization must not merely approve of employee intellectual improvement, it must demand and actively support the educational efforts of all employees regardless of their position in the company. Organizations have routinely offered the option for the intellectual improvement of its management and corporate hierarchy. Since the world is changing as rapidly as it is, this option must be extended to every person on the company payroll because the actions of every person on the company payroll have an impact on the firm. Continuing education is no longer a perk. It is a necessity.

If intellectual improvement is perceived as an option awarded to "The Chosen Few," then disaffection will soon spread throughout the organization. As more employees become involved in continuing their education, the firm, in turn, will reap greater benefits. The greater the employees' stake in the organization's success becomes, their efforts to increase productivity and quality will soon increase as well. No matter how skilled a company's personnel are, unless they (and their organization) move forward together as an intellectual entity, they will eventually be overtaken by their competitors.

The environment in which the organization functions and the organization itself are constantly in flux. No matter how effective or efficient any system is, unless it is consistently and constantly improved upon, the organization will eventually fall behind.

No matter how good an idea is, unless it is continually scrutinized, reworked, and improved, the advantage it gave the organization will disappear.

This will be avoided by continually learning more about oneself, one's skills and talents, the organization itself, customer needs, one's suppliers' procedures and policies, and one's competition. The organization can assist in this undertaking by fostering intellectual improvement at every level in the company.

Getting and staying ahead means the productive use of all knowledge in the organization by all of its members. This is a Learning Organization.

These articles deal with the creation, implementation, and maintenance of a learning organization.

Addleson, Mark. "Organizing to Know and to Learn: Reflections on Organization and Knowledge Management." Srikantaiah, Kanti and Michael E. D. Koenig, eds. *Knowledge Management for the Information Professional*. Medford, NJ: Information Today, 1999.

Argote, Linda et al. "The Persistence and Transfer of Learning in an Industrial Setting." *Management Science* 36.02 (February 1990): 140-154.

Argyris, Chris. "Teaching Smart People How to Learn." *Harvard Business Review* (May-June 1991): 99-109.

Argyris, Chris et al. "The Future of Workplace Learning and Performance." *Training & Development* 48 (May 1994): s36-s47.

Bassi, Laurie et al. "Trends in Workplace Learning: Supply and Demand in Interesting Times." *Training & Development* 52.11 (November 1998): 51-52.

Benson, George. "Battle of the Buzzwords." *Training & Development* 51 (July 1997): 51-52.

Bill, David T. "Transforming EPSS to Support Organizational Learning." *Journal of Instruction Delivery Systems* 11.02 (Spring 1997): 03-11.

Birkner, Lawrence R. and Ruth K. Birkner. "Learning Organization Update: Safety and Health Pros Must Prepare for Careers as Knowledge Workers." *Occupational Hazards* 60.10 (1998): 157.

Brown, J. S. and P. Duguid. "Organizational Learning and Communities-of-Practice: Toward a Unified View of Working." *Organizational Science* 02.01 (1991): 40-57.

Buchanan, Leigh. "Cultivating an Information Culture: Interview with University of Texas Information Systems Management Director Thomas H. Davenport." *CIO* 08.06 (15 December 1994): 46-51.

Burgoyne, John. "Design of the Times." *People Management* 05.11 (03 June 1999): 38-43.

"The Challenge of Managing Organizational Change: Exploring the Relationship of Re-engineering, Developing Learning Organizations and Total Quality Management." *Total Quality Management* 09.01 (February 1998): 109-122.

Cohen, W. and D. Levinthal. "Absorptive Capacity: A New Perspective on Learning and Innovation." *Administrative Science Quarterly* 35 (1990): 128-152.

Collins, Rod. "Auditing in the Knowledge Era." *Internal Auditor* 56.03 (June 1999): 26-31.

Collinson, Simon. "Knowledge Management Capabilities for Steel Makers: A British-Japanese Corporate Alliance for Organizational Learning." *Technology Analysis & Strategic Management* 11.03 (September 1999): 337-358.

"Creating an Agile Learning Organization." *Oil & Gas Journal* (Spring 1999): 30.

Crowley, Bill. "Tacit Knowledge and Quality Assurance: Bridging the Theory-Practice Divide." Srikantaiah, Kanti and Michael E. D. Koenig, eds. *Knowledge Management for the Information Professional*. Medford, NJ: Information Today, 1999.

Darling, Michele S. "Building the Knowledge Organization." *Business Quarterly* 61.02 (Winter 1996): 61-66.

Dysart, Jane I. "Tom Davenport on Knowledge Management: Selected Quotes." *Information Outlook* 01 (June 1997): 27-28.

Eisenberg, Michael B. "Big 6 TIPS: Teaching Information Problem Solving." *Emergency Librarian* 25 (1998).

Elliott, Susan and Carla O'Dell. "Sharing Knowledge & Best Practices: The Hows and Whys of Tapping Your Organization's Hidden Reservoirs of Knowledge." *Health Forum Journal* 42.03 (May-June 1999): 34-37.

Evers, James L. "An Interview with a Utopian Corporate Heretic." *Training & Development* 52.06 (June 1998): 60-64.

Ferguson, Tim W. "Paradigm Change?" *Forbes* (08 March 1999): 90.

Fisher, Kimball and Mareen Duncan Fisher. "Shedding Light on Knowledge Work Learning." *Journal for Quality and Participation* 21.04 (July-August 1998): 08-16.

"FT Knowledge and University of Michigan Business School Announce Groundbreaking Joint Venture for Executive Education." *Business Wire* 1616 (24 January 2000).

Garvin, David A. "Building a Learning Organization." *Harvard Business Review* (July-August 1993): 78-86.

Gauche, Jerry N. "From Media to Markets: A New Paradigm for Information Management." *Records Management Quarterly* 31.04 (October 1997): 03-06.

Gill, T. G. "High-Tech Hidebound: Case Studies of Information Technologies That Inhibited Organizational Learning." *Accounting Management and Information Technologies* 05.01 (1995): 41-60.

Goh, Swee C. "Toward a Learning Organization: The Strategic Building Blocks." *SAM Advanced Management* 63.02 (Spring 1998): 15-22.

Gordon, Jack. "Intellectual Capital and You." *Training* 36.09 (September 1999): 30-38.

Graham, William et al. "A Real-Life Community of Practice." *Training & Development* 52.05 (May 1998): 34-38.

Grayson, Randall. "Excuse Me, Isn't That Your Library on Fire?" *Camping Magazine* 71.05 (September-October 1998): 34-38.

Gregory, Vicki L. "Knowledge Management and Building the Learning Organization." Srikantaiah, Kanti and Michael E. D. Koenig, eds. *Knowledge Management for the Information Professional*. Medford, NJ: Information Today, 1999.

Harrison, Rosemary. "The Contribution of Clinical Directors to the Strategic Capability of the Organization." *British Journal of Management* 10.01 (1999): 23.

"Harvard Business School Opens Portal for Business Community; HBS Working Knowledge Offers Business Information and Research." *Business Wire* 1070 (19 January 2000).

Harvey, Charles and John Denton. "To Come of Age: The Antecedents of Organizational Learning." *Journal of Management Studies* 36.07 (December 1999): 897-918.

Havens, Charnell and Ellen Knapp. "Easing into Knowledge Management." *Strategy & Leadership* 27.02 (March-April 1999): 04-09.

Hennestad, Bjorn W. "For Change Learning." *Human Resources Abstracts* 34.01 (1999).

Hibbard, Justin. "The Learning Revolution." *InformationWeek* 672 (09 March 1998): 44-50.

Hoffmann, S. "Virtual Academies for Companies and Educational Institutions." *Information Services & Use* 19.01: 33-36.

Huber, G. "Organizational Learning: The Contributing Processes and the Literatures." *Organizational Science* 02 (1991): 88-115.

Imai, K. et al. "Managing the New Product Development Process: How Japanese Companies Learn and Unlearn." Clark, K. et al., eds. *The Uneasy Alliance*. Boston: Harvard Business School Press, 1985.

Ives, B. et al. "Integrating Learning Through Knowledge (and Skills) Management." *SIGGROUP Bulletin* 19.01: 51-55.

Jashapara, Ashok. "The Competitive Learning Organization: A Quest for the Holy Grail." *Management Decision* 31.08 (1993): 52-62.

Johannessen, J.-A. et al. "Systemic Thinking as the Philosophical Foundation for Knowledge Management and Organizational Learning." *Kybernetes* 28.01: 24-46.

Kermally, Sultan. "The Learning Organization." *European Management Journal* 15 (April 1997): 208.

Kim, Daniel H. "The Link Between Individual and Organizational Learning." *Sloan Management Review* 35.01 (Fall 1993): 37-50.

King, W. R. "IS and the Learning Organization." *Information Systems Management* 13.03 (Summer 1996): 78-80.

Kinghorn, Jonathan. "U-Turn at Unipart." *Knowledge Directions* 01 (Fall 1999): 06-17.

Klaila, Davis. "Knowledge Management: We Need to Change the Way We Value Work." *Executive Excellence* 17.03 (2000): 13.

Knott, David. "Get Smarter by Sharing Ideas." *Oil & Gas Journal* 95 (26 May 1997): 32-33.

Kouwenhoven, T. "Reengineering for Learning." *SIGGROUP Bulletin* 19.01 39-45.

Levitt, B. and J. G. Marsh. "Organizational Learning." *Annual Review of Sociology* 14 (1988): 319-340.

Liedtka, Jeanne. "Linking Competitive Advantage with Communities of Practice." *Human Resources Abstracts* 34.02 (1999).

Lim, Kwang K. et al. "Managing for Quality through Knowledge Management." *Total Quality Management* 10.04/05 (July 1999): S615-S621.

Lincoln, James R. et al "Organizational Learning and Purchase-Supply Relationships in Japan: Hitachi, Matsushita, and Toyota Compared." *California Management Review Reprint Series* (Spring 1998).

Maule, R. William. "Adult IT Programs: Discourse on Pedagogy, Strategy and the Internet." *Internet Research* 07.02 (1997): 129-152.

McGill, Michael E. and John W. Slocum. "Unlearning the Organization." *Organizational Dynamics* 22.02 (Autumn 1993): 67-78.

Mohanty, R. P. "Evaluating Manufacturing Strategy for a Learning Organization: A Case." *International Journal of Operations and Production Management* 19.03 (1999): 308.

Muralidhar, Sumitra. "Knowledge Management: A Research Scientist's Perspective." Srikantaiah, Kanti and Michael E. D. Koenig, eds. *Knowledge Management for the Information Professional.* Medford, NJ: Information Today, 1999.

Murdoch, Adrian. "Red Brick Revolutionary." *CA Magazine* (February 1999): 28-29.

Nathan, Maria L. "The Nonprofit Executive as Chief Learning Officer." *Nonprofit World* 16.02 (March-April 1998): 39-41.

Pennar, Karen. "The Ties That Lead to Prosperity." *Business Week* (15 December 1997): 153-155.

Reed, M. "Organizations and Modernity: Continuity and Discontinuity in Organization Theory." Hassard, J. and M. Parker, eds. *Postmodernism and Organizations.* London: Sage Publications (1993). 163-182.

Riley, Bryan. "You Are Now Entering the Age of the Mind: Thoughts on the Knowledge Society." *Australian Library Journal* 47.02 (May 1998): 145-156.

Sanchez, R. "Modular Architectures, Knowledge Assets and Organizational Learning: New Management Processes for Product Creation." *International Journal of Technology Management* 19.06 (2000): 610-629.

Sawyer, Steve, et al. "Knowledge Markets: Cooperation Among Distributed Technical Specialists." Srikantaiah, Kanti and Michael E. D. Koenig, eds. *Knowledge Management for the Information Professional*. Medford, NJ: Information Today, 1999.

Senge, Peter. "The Leader's New Work: Building Learning Organizations." *Sloan Management Review* 32.01 (Fall 1990): 07-23.

Senge, Peter. "Rethinking Leadership in the Learning Organization." *The Systems Thinker* 07.01 (1996).

Senge, Peter. "Sharing Knowledge." *Executive Excellence* 15.06 (June 1998): 11-12.

Slocum, John W. et al. "The New Learning Strategy: Anytime, Anything, Anywhere." *Organizational Dynamics* 23.02 (Autumn 1994): 33-47.

Sloman, Martyn. "Seize the Day." *People Management* 05.10 (20 May 1999): 31.

Stamps, David. "Communities of Practice: Learning and Work as Social Activities." *Training* 34 (February 1997): 34-42.

Starbuck, William H. "Learning by Knowledge-Intensive Firms." *Journal of Management Studies* 29.06 (November 1992): 713-740.

Starkey, Ken. "What Can We Learn from a Learning Organization?" *Human Relations* 51.04 (April 1998): 531-546.

Storer, Gary and Cheryl Harris. "Leap of Faith." *People Management* 05.07 (08 April 1999): 58-59.

Szulanski, G. "Intrafirm Transfer of Best Practice, Appropriate Capabilities, Organizational Barriers to Appropriation." Cole, R. *The Death and Life of the American Quality Movement*. New York: Oxford University Press, 1995.

Teece, David J. "Firm Organization, Industrial Structure, and Technological Innovation." *Journal of Economic Behavior and Organization* 31 (1996): 193-224.

Templeton, G. and C. Snyder. "A Model of Organizational Learning Based on Control." *International Journal of Technology Management* (1999): 705-719.

Tetenbaum, Toby J. "Shifting Paradigms: From Newton to Chaos: Part 1 of 2." *Organizational Dynamics* 26.04 (Spring 1998): 21-32.

Tichy, Noel M. and Eli Cohen. "The Teaching Organization." *Training & Development* 52.07 (July 1998): 26-33.

Turoff, R. "An Arranged Marriage: Knowledge Management and Organization Development." *American Programmer* 11.03 (March 1998): 30-33.

Tyre, Marcie J. and Eric Von Hippel. "The Situated Nature of Adaptive Learning in Organizations." *Organization Science* 08.01 (January-February 1997).

Van Fleet, Alanson. "Cultural Anthropology, Storytelling, and Knowledge Management." *Knowledge Directions* 01 (Fall 1999): 78-89.

Wallace, Patricia. "Building the Learning Organization." *KMWorld* 08.09 (September 1999): 28.

Weick, K. E. "Cognitive Processes in Organization." Staw, B., ed. *Research in Organizational Behavior*. Greewich, CT: JAI, 1979.

Yamauchi, Futoshi. "Information, Neighborhood Effects, and the Investment in Human Capital: Learning School Returns in a Dynamic Context." Philadelphia, PA: University of Pennsylvania, Department of Economics, 1998.

Zack, Michael. "Managing Organizational Ignorance." *Knowledge Directions* 01 (Spring 1999): 36-49.

KNOWLEDGE CULTURES/KNOWLEDGE-BASED ORGANIZATIONS

This topic may seem very similar to "Knowledge Management and the Learning Organization,"and it is. But it is not identical. The key word here is "Culture"—the beliefs, conduct, norms, and values that are defined as appropriate behavior by a firm and are encouraged by upper management. Knowledge Management must be integrated into the organizational culture. Unless upper management visibly supports all aspects of a Knowledge Management project, no matter how relevant, useful, and valid a Knowledge Management program is, it will invariably fail because the employees can see that it is not perceived as valuable by the upper echelon.

If a Knowledge Management program is going to be successful, then it must be supported throughout the entire organization. Any organizational changes must be adopted by the organizational culture as a whole in order to be successful. Organization-wide acceptance of change is the single most difficult, the most expensive, and the most time-consuming stage in the process. The difficulty lies in the fact that most humans do not like change, especially if the organization is going back to the old ways eventually. "This one will go away after six months just like (choose your acronym)." Trying to adapt to change can be a traumatic event—especially after all of the build-up that traditionally precedes it. Factor in the pressure created because the change comes from the Executive Suite, and this situation can become unbearable—especially if the change that is recommended fails from lack of support from those who initiated it. In extreme cases, employees will become apathetic and disaffected.

As rapidly as the business world is moving today, an organization must accept and support Knowledge Management throughout its entire structure—not just in the "Information Technology,""Knowledge Management," or "Technical Services" departments. Knowledge creation and sustenance are essential. The culture of the organization must change and support the Knowledge Culture. In order to be successful, Knowledge Management must be an organizational imperative. If not, an organization can miss an opportunity that will break the company.

Birkinshaw, Julian. "Acquiring Intellect: Managing the Integration of Knowledge-Intensive Acquisitions." *Business Horizons* 42.03 (May-June 1999): 33-40.

Blair, Jim. "Knowledge Management: The Era of Shared Ideas." *Forbes* (22 September 1997): 28.

Boland, R. J., Jr. and R. V. Tenkasi. "Perspective Making and Perspective Taking in Communities of Knowing." *Organization Science* 06.03 (1995): 350-372.

Bonaventura, M. "The Benefits of a Knowledge Culture." *ASLIB Proceedings* 49.04 (April 1997): 82-89.

Caulkin, Simon. "So, a Little Knowledge Is Not Quite So Dangerous." *The Observer* (28 September 1997): B10.

Coleman, David. "Collaboration and Knowledge Management Theory and Practice." *Knowledge Management Review* 05 (November-December 1998): 16-21.

Coleman, David. "Hot Tip Collaboration and Knowledge Management: Findings from a New Study." http://www.collaborate.com/tip.html (08 September 1997).

Coles, Margaret. "Knowing Is Succeeding." *Director* 52.08 (March 1999): 60-63.

"Collaborative Knowledge." *Human Resource Planning* 22.01 (1999): 22-23.

"Communicating Best Practices: How to Facilitate Knowledge Sharing in All Levels of Your Organization." *Business Wire* 1599 (03 February 2000).

"Creating an Agile Learning Organization." *Oil & Gas Journal* (Spring 1999): 30.

Darling, Michele S. "Knowledge Cultures." *Executive Excellence* 14.02 (February 1997): 10-11.

Darling, Michele S. "The Knowledge Organization: A Journey Worth Taking." *Vital Speeches of the Day* (10 June 1996): 693-697.

Dash, Julekha. "Knowledge Is Power." *Software Magazine* 18.01 (January 1998): 46-56.

Davis, Stan and Jim Botkin. "The Coming of Knowledge-Based Business." Neef, Dale, ed. *The Knowledge Economy*. Boston: Butterworth-Heinmann, 1998.

De Meyer, Arnoud. "Manufacturing Operations in Europe: Where Do We Go Next?" *European Management Journal* 16.03 (June 1998): 262-271.

Dixon, Nancy. "The Insight Track." *People Management* 06.04 (17 February 2000): 34-39.

Dove, Rick. "Implementing Stealth Knowledge Management." *Automotive Manufacturing & Production* 111.06 (June 1999): 16-17.

Dove, Rick. "Outsourcing Knowlege Work—Why Not?" *Automotive Manufacturing & Production* 111.10 (October 1999): 16-17.

Drucker, Peter F. "The Age of Social Transformation." *The Atlantic* 274.05 (November 1997): 53-70.

Drucker, Peter F. "The Coming of Knowledge-Based Business." *Harvard Business Review* 66.01 (September-October 1988): 45-53.

Eckhouse, John. "Get Creative with Knowledge Sharing." *InformationWeek* 720 (08 February 1999): 19ER.

Eckhouse, John. "Sharing Knowledge Isn't Easy Yet." *InformationWeek* 748 (16 August 1999): 99.

Evans, Bob. "A Culture of Innovation." *InformationWeek* 725 (15 March 1999): 10.

Evans, Bob. "Imagine the Possibilities." *InformationWeek* 752 (September 13, 1999): 10.

Find, Soren. "Changing the Culture—Job Design, Work Processes and Qualifications in the Hybrid Library." *IFLA Journal* 25.04 (1999): 237-239.

Floyd, Steven W. and Bill Woolridge. "Knowledge Creation and Social Networks in Corporate Entrepreneurship: The Renewal of Organizational Capability." *Entrepreneurship: Theory & Practice* 23.03 (Spring 1999): 123-143.

Gammack, J.G. and P. R. Goulding. "Ethical Responsibility and the Management of Knowledge." *Australian Computer Journal* 31.03 (August 1999): 72-77.

Glasser, Perry. "The Knowledge Factor." *CIO* 12.06 (15 December 1998-01 January 1999): 108-118.

Grant, Robert M. "The Knowledge-Based View of the Firm: Implications for Management Practice." *Long Range Planning* 30.03 (June 1997): 450-454.

Grant, Robert M. "Toward a Knowledge-Based Theory of the Firm." *Strategic Management Journal* 17 (Winter 1996): 109-122.

Gupta, Anil K. and Vijay Govindarajan. "Knowledge Flows within Multinational Corporations." *Strategic Management Journal* 21.04 (April 2000): 473-496.

Hackbarth, Gary and Varun Grover. "The Knowledge Repository: Organizational Memory Information Systems." *Information Systems Management* 16.03 (Summer 1999): 21-30.

Hanley, Susan S. "A Culture Built on Sharing." *InformationWeek* 731 (26 April 1999): 16ER-17ER.

Harris, David. "Creating a Knowledge-Centric Information Technology Environment." http://www.htcs.com/ckc.htm

Hiser, Jeff. "Understanding the Value of Your Employees' Knowledge." *CPA Journal* 68.07 (July 1998): 56-57.

Holsapple, Clyde W. and Andrew B. Whinston. "Knowledge-Based Organizations." *Information Society* 05.02 (1987): 77-90.

Koudsi, Suzanne. "Actually, It Is Like Brain Surgery: Bruce Strong Dreamed up Fancy Technology to Help Employees Share Ideas. Then Came the Tough Part: Persuading Them to Use the Stuff." *Fortune* 141.06 (20 March 2000).

Larson, Melissa. "Replacing the Quality Craftsman." *Quality* 38.05 (April 1999): 48-51.

Lei, David et al. "Designing Organizations for Competitive Advantage: The Power of Unlearning and Learning." *Organizational Dynamics* 27.03 (Winter 1999): 24-38.

Maloney, John T. "Knowledge Transfer Is Critical to ERP Success." *KMWorld* 08.04 (April 1999): 59, 60.

Marshall, Michael P. "Managing Your Company's Knowledge." *Agency Sales* 30.01 (January 2000): 41-42.

Martinez, Michelle Neely. "Knowledge Management: The Collective Power." *HR Magazine* 43 (February 1998): 88-92, 94.

Master, Melissa. "Making It Work: How Leading Companies Are Tapping into the Knowledge of Their Workforce." *Across the Board* 36.08 (September 1999): 21-24.

Mazzie, Mark. "Mind Melds." *CIO* 13.02 (15 October 1999): 86-90.

McDermott, Richard and Carla O'Dell. "Overcoming the 'Cultural Barriers' to Sharing Knowledge." http://www.apqc.org/free/articles/km0200/

Meister, Jeanne C. "Extending the Short Shelf Life of Knowledge." *Training & Development* 52.06 (01 June 1998): 52.

Neef, Dale. "Making the Case for Knowledge Management: The Bigger Picture." 37.01 (1999): 72.

Nonaka, Ikujiro. "A Dynamic Theory of Organizational Knowledge Creation." *Organization Science* 05.01 (February 1994): 14-37.

Nonaka, Ikujiro. "The Knowledge-Creating Company." *Harvard Business Review* (November-December 1991): 96-99.

Nonaka, Ikujiro. "A Theory of Organizational Knowledge Creation." *International Journal of Technology Management* 11.07-08 (1996): 833-845.

Nonaka, Ikujiro and Noboru Konno. "The Concept of 'Ba': Building a Foundation for Knowledge Creation." *California Management Review* 40.03 (Spring 1998): 40-54.

O'Dell, Carla. "Knowledge Tranfer: Discover Your Value Proposition." *Strategy & Leadership* 27.02 (March-April 1999): 10-15.

Olson, John A. "What Academic Librarians Should Know about Creative Thinking." *The Journal of Academic Librarianship* 25.05 (September 1999): 383-389.

Orr, J. "Sharing Knowledge, Celebrating Identity, Community Memory in a Service Culture." Middleton, D., and D. Edwards, eds. *Collective Remembering.* Newbury Park: Sage (1990). 169-189.

Ostro, Nilly. "Dynamics." *Chief Executive* 123 (May 1997): 62.

Pennar, Karen. "The Ties That Lead to Prosperity." *Business Week* (15 December 1997): 153-155.

"The People Factor." *People Management* 04.02 (22 January 1998): 38.

Pfeffer, Jeffrey. "Seven Practices of Successful Organizations, Part 2: Invest in Training, Reduce Status Differences, Don't Keep Secrets." *Health Forum Journal* 42.02 (March-April 1999): 55-57.

Phillips, Tim. "The Truth about Sharing Knowledge." *Director* 52.12 (July 1999): 75.

Powell, Tim. "Competitive Knowledge Management: You Can't Reengineer What Never Was Engineered in the First Place." *Competitive Intelligence Review* 08.01 (Spring 1997): 40-47.

Robertson, Maxine and Geraldine O'Malley Hammersley. "Knowledge Management Practices within a Knowledge-Intensive Firm: The Significance of the People Management Dimension." *Journal of European Industrial Training* 24.02, 04 (27 April 2000): 241-253.

Salopek, Jennifer J. and Nancy M. Dixon. "Common Knowledge: How Companies Thrive by Sharing What They Know." *Training & Development* 54.04 (April 2000): 63.

Scarbrough, Harry. "System Error." *People Management* 05.07 (08 April 1999): 68-70.

Shulman, Seth. "We Need New Ways to Own and Share Knowledge." *The Chronicle of Higher Education* 45.24 (19 February 1999): A64.

Silver, Bruce. "Walking the Walk." *KMWorld* 07.03 (16 March 1998): 24-25.

Skyrme, David J. and Debra Amidon. "Creating the Knowledge-Based Business." http://www.skyrme.com/pubs/kmreport.htm

Spender, J. C. "Making Knowledge the Basis of a Dynamic Theory of the Firm." *Strategic Management Journal* 17 (Winter 1996): 45-62.

Spender, J. C. and R. M. Grant. "Knowledge and the Firm: Overview." *Strategic Management Journal* 17 (1996): 45-62.

Storck, John and Patricia A. Hill. "Knowledge Diffusion through 'Strategic Communities'." *Sloan Management Review* 41.02 (Winter 2000): 63-74.

Suddaby, Roy R. "Knowledge as Culture: The New Sociology of Knowledge." *International Journal of Organizational Analysis* 07.01 (January 1999): 93-95.

Sunoo, Brenda Paik. "Culture Drives Knowledge Sharing." *Workforce* 78.03 (March 1999): 34.

Sunoo, Brenda Paik. "How HR Supports Knowledge Sharing." *Workforce* 78.03 (March 1999): 30.

Tobin, Daniel R. "Networking Your Knowledge." *Management Review* 87.04 (April 1998): 46-48.

Tsoukas, Haridmos. "The Firm as a Distributed Knowledge System: A Constructionist Approach." *Strategic Management Journal* 17 (Winter 1996): 11-25.

Verespej, Mike. "Knowledge Management: System or Culture?" *Industry Week* 248.15 (16 August 1999): 20.

Vogl, A. J. "One Big Story." *Across the Board* 36.08 (September 1999): 01.

Von Krogh, Georg et al. "Develop Knowledge Activists!" *European Management Journal* 15.05 (October 1997): 475-483.

Waitley, Denis. "Self Leadership and Change." *Empires of the Mind: Lessons to Lead and Succeed in a Knowledge-Based World*. New York: William Morrow, 1995.

Watt, Peggy. "Interview—Q & A: Where Learning Counts." *Network World* 14 (18 August 1997): I23-I24.

Webber, Alan M. "Surviving in the New Economy." *Harvard Business Review* (September-October 1994): 76.

Webber, Alan M. "What's So New About the New Economy?" *Harvard Business Review* (January-February 1993): 24.

Welles, Edward O. "Mind Gains." *Inc* 21.18 (December 1999).

Wilkinson, Barry A. "Sharing Knowledge Pays off." *Best's Review* 100.09 (January 2000): 113.

White, Janet. "The New Work Order." *Benefits Canada* 23.06 (June 1999): 21.

Yavuz, Ed M. and Daniel Heidelman. "Knowledge Management: The 'Office Water Cooler' of the 21st Century." *Medical Marketing & Media* 34.04 (April 1999): 66-70.

Zuboff, S. "The Emperor's New Workplace." *Scientific American* 273.03 (September 1995): 202-204.

KNOWLEDGE MAPPING/INFORMATION AUDIT

Knowledge is everywhere. The $64,000 questions are: where is it, who has it, and how do we get it to those who need it when they need it? The Knowledge Map/Information Audit are two ways that will assure a company a proper beginning to its Knowledge Management program. Haphazard application of any new system will cause the system to fail, regardless of the quality of the system. To implement a Knowledge Management program properly, much groundwork must be done in terms of changing the organizational culture. Since this is the most difficult and lengthy process of the implementation procedure, it must be started first. The Knowledge Map/Information Audit is the next step toward the goal. If The Knowledge Map/Information Audit is not done prior to any computer, network, or personnel changes, then all of the effort, resources, and time will be wasted. How will the new systems be selected, and by whom? Who will have access to which parts of the system? Who is best suited to oversee each section? These questions are best answered by a Knowledge Map/Information Audit. Unless a company has unlimited resources, a Knowledge Map/Information Audit is an absolute necessity.

The ultimate objective of Knowledge Management is to get the necessary knowledge to the people who can best apply it in time for it to have a positive impact on the organization. Knowledge managers are generally familiar with the systems and infrastructure since they often have a hand in its creation. They are also very likely to know what specific knowledge is located where and with whom. What about the other employees in the organization who are expected to contribute to and use Knowledge Management? The Knowledge Map/Information Audit can also provide valuable information to other members of the organization who access the knowledge as a prerequisite to performing their jobs.

The Knowledge Map/Information Audit is a way for an organization to not only see where it is in terms of its Knowledge Management program, but also assist in planning its future development. While the Information Audit can indicate shortfalls in performance, it can also indicate where the organizational performance has exceeded expectations.

Babiera, A. M. "Knowledge Management and the EBRD: Designing a Knowledge Management Programme for the Office of the Chief Economist." *ASLIB Proceedings: New Information Perspectives* 51.07: 233-242.

Bates, Mary Ellen. "Information Audits: What Do We Know and When Do We Know It?" *Library Management Briefings* (Fall 1997).

Berkman, Robert. "The Steps to Take for Conducting an Information Audit." *Information Advisor Knowledge Management Quarterly Supplement* 01.03 (September 1997): 01-04.

Buchanan, S. and F. Gibb. "The Information Audit: An Integrated Strategic Approach." *International Journal of Information Management* 18.01 (February 1998): 29-47.

Chen, J. "The Natural Structure of Scientific Knowledge: An Attempt to Map a Knowledge Structure." *Journal of Information Science* 14.03 (1998): 131-140.

Chmielewski, T. L. and D. F. Dansereau. "Enhancing the Recall of Text: Knowledge Mapping Training Promotes Implicit Transfer." *Journal of Educational Psychology* 90.03 (September 1998): 407-413.

Chuck, Lysbeth B. "For a Really Good Time, Call Your Digital Information Manager." *Searcher: The Magazine for Database Professionals* (01 October 1998): 69.

Chung, G. K. W. K. et al. "The Use of Computer-Based Collaborative Knowledge Mapping to Measure Team Processes and Team Outcomes." *Computers in Human Behaviour* 15.03-04 (1999): 463-493.

Cliffe, Sarah. "Knowledge Management: The Well-Connected Business." *Harvard Business Review* 76.04 (July-August 1998): 17-21.

Cortez, Edwin and Edward Kazlauskas. "Information Policy Audit: A Case Study of an Organizational Analysis Tool." *Special Libraries* (Spring 1996): 85-88.

Crandell, Thomas L. et al. "Empirical Evaluation of Concept Mapping: A Job Performance Aid for Writers." *Technical Communication* 43.02 (May 1996): 157-163.

Despres, C. and C. Danade. "How to Map Knowledge Management." *The Financial Times* (08 March 1999): 01.

Dietrick, Bill. "The Art of Knowledge Mapping: Where to Begin." *Information Advisor Knowledge Management Supplement* 01.04 (December 1997): 01-03.

Drucker, Peter F. "Beyond the Information Revolution." *The Atlantic Monthly* 284.04 (October 1999): 47-57.

Esque, Timm J. "Knowledge Mapping: A Multipurpose Task Analysis Tool." *Journal of Instructional Development* 11.04 (1988): 39-50.

Gibb, F. and S. Buchanan. "The Information Audit: An Integrated Strategic Approach." *International Journal of Information Management* 18.01 (February 1998): 29-47.

Herl, H. E. et al. "Reliability and Validity of a Computer-Based Knowledge Mapping System to Measure Content Understanding." *Computers in Human Behaviour* 15.03-04 (1999): 315-333.

Hildebrand, Carol. "Guiding Principles." *CIO* 08.18 (July 1995): 60-64.

Horton, F. W. Jr. "Knowledge Mapping: A Window of Opportunity." *SLA Specialist* 19.01 (January 1996): 01-14.

Horton, F. W. Jr. "Mapping Corporate Information Resources." *International Journal of Information Management* 08.04 (1988): 249-259.

Horton, F. W. Jr. "Mapping Corporate Information Resources." *International Journal of Information Management* 09.01 (1989): 19-24.

Horton, F. W. Jr. "Mapping Corporate Information Resources." *International Journal of Information Management* 09.02 (1989): 91-95.

"The Information Audit." *Information Advisor* 07.01 (January 1995): 02.

"Information Overload: The Information Audit." *Information Advisor* 07.01 (January 1995): 02.

Jeffrey, Gundi. "Measuring the Intangible." *The Accountant* 59.27 (November 1997): 13-15.

Liu, C.-M. "New Characteristic of Information Systems." *Journal of Information, Communication, and Library Science* 04.02 (Winter 1997): 14-18.

McCagg, Edward C. and Donald F. Dansereau. "A Convergent Paradigm for Examining Knowledge Mapping as a Learning Strategy." *Journal of Educational Research* 84.06 (July-August 1991): 317-324.

Murray, B. S. and E. McDaid. "Visualizing and Representing Knowledge for the End User: A Review." *International Journal of Machine Studies* 38 (1993): 23-49.

Ostro, Nilly. "Metrics." *Chief Executive* 123 (May 1997): 61.

Reynolds, S. B. and D. F. Dansereau. "The Knowledge Hypermap: An Alternative to Hypertext." *Computers & Education* 14.05 (1990): 409-416.

Rossett, Allison. "Knowledge Management Meets Analysis." *Training & Development* 53.05 (May 1999): 62-68.

Skyrme, D. J. "Valuing Knowledge: Is It Worth It?" *Managing Information* 05.03 (March 1998): 24-26.

Strassmann, Paul A. "Managing: Taking the Measure of Knowledge Assets." *ComputerWorld* 32 (06 April 1998): 73-75.

Stewart, Thomas A. "Measuring Company IQ." *Fortune* 120 (24 January 1994): 24.

Stewart, Thomas A. "Mapping Corporate Brainpower." *Fortune* 132.09 (30 October 1995): 209-212.

Taha, I. A. and J. Ghosh. "Symbolic Interpretation of Artificial Neural Networks." *IEEE Transactions on Knowledge and Data Engineering* 11.03: 448-463.

"A Talk with...Bipin Junnarkar." *Information Advisor* 09.12 (December 1997): S4.

Tessmer, M. "Meeting with the SME to Design Multimedia Exploration Systems." *Educational Technology, Research and Development* 46.02 (1998): 79-95.

Tsai, Bor-sheng. "Infomapping in Information Retrieval." Srikantaiah, Kanti and Michael E. D. Koenig, eds. *Knowledge Management for the Information Professional*. Medford, NJ: Information Today, 1999.

Vail, Edmond F. "Knowledge Mapping: Getting Started with Knowledge Management." *Information Systems Management* 16.04 (Fall 1999): 16-23.

Wiggs, Cheri L. and Ray S. Perez. "The Use of Knowledge Acquisition in Instructional Design." *Computers in Human Behavior* 04.03 (1988): 257-274.

KNOWLEDGE MANAGEMENT AND ITS ORGANIZATIONAL ASPECTS

Human beings do not like change. Large groups of humans (like organizations, for example), like change even less. Therefore, whenever a new discipline comes along, there is stiff resistance to implementing it. "Things are just fine the way they are." "Once we get used to one thing, they start another." The implementation of change is made more difficult when concrete evidence of its value is slow in coming, or even worse, the results of the change are hard to quantify.

Knowledge Management is a process, a perpetual process. Unlike a monthly Income Statement or a product run, it has no end. It is a continuing, evolving function that changes to meet the changing needs of the organization as the organization and its internal and external environments change. Knowledge Management is not a department within the organization. It is, rather, a function that permeates the organization. From the Finance Department to the shop floor, Knowledge Management reaches out to and connects all departments, thus making the organization more focused. The time of an individual working in a vacuum is long gone. Knowledge Management facilitates the pooling of assets from individual departments throughout the organization. Rather than the group that has information determining if anyone could use it, Knowledge Management makes it available to all. Allowing everyone who might need these insights to determine whether or not something can or cannot be modified to meet their needs.

Knowledge must be explicitly managed. This concept does not mean that once the system is started that it is a static proposition. The system must also be amenable to change because change permeates the organization and its environments.

Therefore, it is absolutely essential that it be supported throughout the organization—from upper management to the newest recruit. If the organization does not fully and absolutely support Knowledge Management, then it will become yet another failed management fad. Knowledge Management has value, it has uses for every organization everywhere, regardless of the type of business the organization does.

In any organization, it is not difficult to see what project(s) have the support of senior management. These are the projects that get everyone's greatest effort in order to make them succeed, they are the ones most talked about, the ones that receive the most attention throughout the organization as well as the best financial backing. Knowledge Management, especially in the beginning, must also have this type of continual and absolute support. Once the Knowledge Management program is up and running, it is crucial that it still receives the attention and support (of all kinds) from the upper echelon. As the Knowledge Management program achieves some successes and proves its worth, then the organization will be won over to its side.

These articles describe different strategies for making Knowledge Management an organizational imperative, not just a departmental one.

Abecker, A. et al. "Toward a Technology for Organizational Memories." *IEEE Intelligent Systems* 13.03 (May-June 1998): 40-48.

Ackerman, Mark S. and Christine A. Halverson. "Reexamining Organizational Memory." *Communications of the ACM* 43.01 (January 2000): 58-64.

Alonzo, Vincent and Daniel McQuillen. "Best Corporate Asset: Brain Power?" *Incentive* 170.01 (January 1996): 07.

Anthes, Gary H. "Learning How to Share." *ComputerWorld* 32 (23 February 1998): 75-78.

Ayers, J. "A Primer on Supply-Chain Management." *Information Strategy: The Executive's Journal* 16.02 (Winter 2000): 06-15.

Balisani, Ettore and Enrico Scarso. "Information Technology Management: A Knowledge-Based Perspective." *Technovation* 19.04 (April 1999): 209-217.

Barr, P. S. et al. "Cognitive Change, Strategic Action and Organizational Renewal." *Strategic Management Journal* 17 (1996): 15-36.

Barucci, Emilio. "Differential Games with Nonconvexities and Positive Spillovers." *European Journal of Operational Research* 121.01 (15 February 2000): 193-204.

Battisti, Michele. "Information and Knowledge Management in Tomorrow's Enterprise: The Dynamic Role of Information Activities." *Documentaliste* 36.01 (January-February 1999): 18-20.

Blackler, F. "Knowledge, Knowledge Work, and Organizations: An Overview and Interpretation." *Organization Studies* 16.06 (1995).

Blair, Jim and R. Hunter. "Introducing the KM Project Viability Assessment." *Research Note KM: SPA-03-5005* Stamford, CT: Gartner Group, 1998.

Brass, D. J. "Being in the Right Place: A Structural Analysis of Individual Influence in an Organization." *Administrative Science Quarterly* 29 (1984): 518-539.

Breton, Ernest J. "Creating a Corporate Brain." *Bulletin of the American Society for Information Science* 15.01 (October-November 1988): 27-28.

Brown, John Seely and Paul Duguid. "Organizing Knowledge." *California Management Review Reprint Series* (Spring 1998).

Brown, Reva Berman and Martyn J. Woodland. "Managing Knowledge Wisely: A Case Study in Organisational Behaviour." *Journal of Applied Management Studies* 02 (December 1999): 175-198.

Browning, John. "Teaching Old Dogs New Tricks." *New Statesman* (27 September 1999): R11-R12.

Brubaker, Steve. "Promoting from Within: The Best Way to Build Management." *Fund Raising Management* 30.08 (October 1999): 40-42.

Caggiano, Christopher. "Low-Tech Smarts: Knowledge Management Isn't Just for Big Companies Anymore." *Inc.* 21.01 (January 1999): 79-80.

Callison, Daniel. "Knowledge Management." *School Library Media Activities Monthly* 16.07 (March 2000): 37-39, 45.

Carayannia, Elias G. "Fostering Synergies between Information Technology and Managerial and Organizational Cognition: The Role of Knowledge Management." *Technovation* 19.04 (April 1999): 219.

Cates, Jo A. "Sharing Knowledge on Knowledge." *Business & Finance Division Bulletin* 112 (Fall 1999): 43-46.

Chapman, Christy. "A Melding of the Minds." *Internal Auditor* 56.03 (June 03, 1999): 06.

Chen, Rui. "The Eighth Stage of Knowledge Management: Information Services Management (IRM) vs. Knowledge Management (KM), and the Chief Information Officer (CIO) vs. the Chief Knowledge Officer (CKO)." *International Forum on Information and Documentation* 23.01 (1998): 18-24.

"Chiseling Building Blocks of Corporate Expertise; Complexity Meets Collaboration." *Chemical Week* (19 January 2000): 32.

Choo, C. W. "The Intelligent Organization: Mobilizing Organizational Knowledge through Information Partnerships." Faculty of Information Studies, University of Toronto (1999).

Coleman, David. "Taking the Best Approach to Knowledge Management." *Computer Reseller News* 791 (01 June 1998): 111-112.

Comeau-Kirschner, Cheryl. "The Sharing Culture." *Management Review* (January 2000): 08.

"Custom KM: Implementing the Right Knowledge Management Strategy for Your Organization." *Cutter IT Journal* 12.11 (November 1999): 06-14.

Dannhauser, Carol Leonetti. "Plugging the Brain Drain: Learning to Share May Be the Secret." *Working Woman* 24.10 (November 1999): 40-41.

Davenport, Thomas H. "Knowledge Management Case Study." *Knowledge Management at Ernst & Young 1997.*

Davenport, Thomas H. "Putting the Enterprise into the Enterprise System." *Harvard Business Review* 76.04 (July-August 1998): 121-131.

Davenport, Thomas H. et al. "Improving Processes for Knowledge Work." *Chemtech* 26.10 (October 1996): 14-23.

Debons, Anthony. "Knowledge Counseling: The Concept, the Process, and Its Application." Srikantaiah, Kanti and Michael E. D. Koenig, eds. *Knowledge Management for the Information Professional.* Medford, NJ: Information Today, 1999.

DeCarolis, Donna Marie et al. "The Impact of Stocks and Flows of Organizational Knowledge on Firm Performance: An Empirical Investigation of the Biotechnology Industry." *Strategic Management Journal* 20.10 (October 1999): 953-968.

DiMattia, S. S. and L. C. Blumenstein. "Virtual Libraries: Meeting the Corporate Challenge." *Library Journal* 124.04: 42-44.

Dove, Rick. "Agility = Knowledge Management + Response Ability." *Automotive Manufacturing & Production* 111.03 (March 1999): 16-17.

Dove, Rick. "The Avoidance of Knowledge Management." *Automotive Manufacturing & Production* 111.05 (May 1999): 16-17.

Dove, Rick. "Fishing for Knowledge." *Automotive Manufacturing & Production* 111.02 (February 1999): 22-23.

Dove, Rick. "Managing Core Competency Knowledge." *Automotive Manufacturing and Production* 109.12 (December 1997): 18-19.

Dove, Rick. "Managing the Knowledge Portfolio." *Automotive Manufacturing & Production* 111.04 (April 1999): 16-17.

Due, R. T. "The Eye of the Beholder: A Third Approach to Knowledge Management." *American Programmer* 11.03 (March 1998): 26-29.

Edwards, Ray. "KM & the Human Element." *KMWorld* 07.06 (11 May 2000): 46-47.

Elliott, S. "Arthur Andersen Maximizes Its Core Commodity through Comprehensive Knowledge Management." *Practice* (August-September 1997): 01-07.

Empson, L. "Fear of Exploitation and Fear of Association: Exploring Impediments to Knowledge Transfer in Mergers Between Professional Services Firms." (1999).

Ernst & Young. "Mastering Information Management." *The Financial Times* (08 March 1999).

Evink, Janis R. and Henry H. Beam. "Just What Is an Ideation Group?" *Business Horizons* 42.01 (January-February 1999): 73-78.

"Fading Fads." *Economist* 355.8167 (22 April 2000): 60-61.

Fahey, Liam. "Scenarios and Knowledge." *Knowledge Directions* 01 (Spring 1999): 50-59.

Fan, I. S. et al. "Supplier Knowledge Exchange in Aerospace Product Engineering." *Aircraft Engineering and Aerospace Technology* 72.01 (2000): 14-17.

Foster, Faren. "How to Make Communities Work for You." *KMWorld* 08.02 (February 1999): 35.

Frappaolo, Carl. "Search and Retrieval Lay the Foundation to Knowledge Discovery." *KMWorld* 07.06 (11 May 2000): 28, 31, 34.

Garrett, Alexander. "Crash Course: Knowing What You Know." *Management Today* (November 1999): 132.

Gautschi, Ted. "Knowledge as Advantage." *Design News* 54.15 (02 August 1999): 156.

Grayson, C. Jackson, Jr. and Carla S. O'Dell. "Horse and Carriage: Benchmarking and Knowledge Management." *Across the Board* 35.04 (April 1998): 25.

Griffiths, Jose-Marie. "Track 5: Social, Behavioral, Cultural and Ethical Factors, Part 1." *Bulletin of the American Society for Information Science* 26.02 (December 1999-January 2000): 21-22.

Grinyer, P. and P. McKiernan. "Generating Major Change in Stagnating Companies." *Strategic Management Journal* (1990): 131-146.

Hamilton, Feona. "Know Wonder." *Accountancy* 124.1273 (September 1999): 44-45.

Hargadon, Andrew. "Firms as Knowledge Brokers: Lessons in Pursuing Continuous Innovation." *California Management Review Reprint Series* (Spring 1998).

Harney, J. "CRM Workflow: Knowledge Management with a Backbone." *Intelligent Enterprise* 02.13 (14 September 1999): 28-30, 32, 34-35.

Harrison, Roy. "Need to Know." *People Management* 05.03 (11 February 1999): 31.

Havens, Charnell and Edward E. Gordon. "How to Identify and Clone Top Performers." *Corporate University Review* 06.02 (March 1998): 42-45.

Hedlund, Gunnar. "A Model of Knowledge Management and the N-Form Corporation." *Strategic Management Journal* 15 (Summer 1994): 73-90.

Hiebeler, Robert J. "Benchmarking: Knowledge Management." *Strategy and Leadership* 24.02 (March-April 1996): 22-29.

Hoard, Bruce. "People Haven't Contributed to the Collective." *KMWorld* 06.16 (17 November 1997): 45.

Holsapple, C. W. "Knowledge Management in Decision Making and Decision Support." *Knowledge and Policy* 08.01 (Spring 1995): 05-22.

"How to Succeed in the New Knowledge Economy: Linking Knowledge Management to Corporate Strategy." *Business Wire* 1541 (31 January 2000).

Huhns, M. N. and L. M. Stephens. "Personal Ontologies." *IEEE Internet Computing* 03.05 (September-October 1999): 85-87.

"Intellectual Capital: Trendsetter: John Hokkanen." *Law Practice Management* 25.05 (July-August 1999): 44.

"It's What You Know and Share That Counts." *Training* 34.02 (February 1997): 18-20.

Johannessen, Jon-Alrid et al. "Aspects of Innovation Theory Based on Knowledge Management." *International Journal of Information Management* (April 1999): 121.

Johnson, Donald E. L. "Knowledge Management Is New Competitive Edge." *Health Care Strategic Management* 16.07 (July 1998): 02-03.

"Just the Facts: Knowledge is Money." *Journal of Business Strategy* 20.06 (November 1999): 04.

Kampffmeyer, U. and S. Werther. "Knowledge Is Power, But Only When It Is Shared: On the State of Knowledge Management in Business." *NFD Information-Wissenschaft und Praxis* 50.03: 142-148.

Keeler, Janice. "Track 5: Social, Behavioral, Cultural and Ethical Factors, Part 2." *Bulletin of the American Society for Information Science* 26.02 (December 1999-January 2000): 22-23.

Kerr, S. "Creating the Boundaryless Organization: The Radical Reconstruction of Organization Capabilities." *Planning Review* (September-October 1995): 41-45.

Kim, W. C. and R. Maubourgne. "Fair Process: Managing in the Knowledge Economy." *Harvard Business Review* 75.04: 65-75.

Kim, W. Chan and Renee Mauborgne. "Strategy, Value Innovation, and the Knowledge Economy." *Sloan Management Review* 40.03 (Spring 1999): 41.

Knapp, Ellen. "Easing into Knowledge Management." *Strategy & Leadership* 27.02 (March-April 1999): 04-09.

"Know Thyself." *Industry Week* 249.02 (24 January 2000): 08.

Koenig, M. E. D. and T. D. Wilson. "Productivity Growth, the Take-Off Point." *Information Processing and Management* 32.02: 247-254.

Kogut, B. and U. Zander. "Knowledge of the Firm, Combinative Capabilities, and the Replication of Technology." *Organization Science* 03 (1992): 383-397.

Krohn, U. et al. "Concept Lattices for Knowledge Management." *BT Technology Journal* 17.04 (October 1999): 108-116.

Lahti, Ryan K. and Michael M. Beyerlein. "Knowledge Transfer and Management Consulting: A Look at 'The Firm'." *Business Horizons* 43.01 (January-February 2000).

Lesser, Eric. "White Paper: Communities of Practice: Realizing the Benefits." IBM Institute for Knowledge Management, April 1999.

Lesser, Eric and Laurence Prusak. "Spotlight on Knowledge Management: Developing a Strategy to Improve Organizational Effectiveness." Cortada, James W. and John A. Woods, eds. *The Quality Yearbook: 1998 Edition.* New York: McGraw-Hill, 1998.

Lesser, Eric and Laurence Prusak. "Using Performance Measures to Build Organizational Knowledge." Cortada, James W. and John A. Woods, eds. *The 1998 ASTD Training and Performance Yearbook.* New York: McGraw-Hill, 1998.

Lesser, Eric and Laurence Prusak. "White Paper: Communities of Practice, Social Capital and Organizational Knowledge." IBM Institute for Knowledge Management, August 1999.

Liebeskind, J. P. "Knowledge, Strategy, and the Theory of the Firm." *Strategic Management Journal* 17 (1996): 93-108.

Liedtka, J. M. et al. "The Generative Cycle: Linking Knowledge and Relationships." *Sloan Management Review* 39.01: 47-59.

Malloy, Amy. "Supporting Knowledge Management: You Have It Now." *Computerworld* 32 (23 February 1998): 78.

Malone, Thomas W. et al. "Tools for Inventing Organizations: Toward a Handbook of Organizational Processes." *Management Science* 45.03 (March 1999): 425.

Maloney, John T. "Communities of Practice: Five Factors for Success." *KMWorld* 08.02 (February 1999): 35.

Mann, Tommy. "Knowledge Management." *Chemical Market Reporter* 257.03 (17 January 2000): 13.

McCartney, Laton. "Getting Smart About Knowledge Management: Managing Intellectual Resources Can Maximize Innovation and Competitiveness." *Industry Week* 247.09 (04 May 1998): 30-34.

Miles, Raymond E. et al. "Organizing in the Knowledge Age: Anticipating the Cellular Form." *Academy of Management Review* 11 (November 1997): 07-20.

Milstead, Jessica. "Track 2: Classification and Representation." *Bulletin of the American Society for Information Science* 26.02 (December 1999-January 2000): 13-15.

Moore, Connie. "Eureka! Xerox Discovers Way to Grow Community Knowledge." *KMWorld* 08.10 (October 1999): 10-11.

Murray, Gerry and Arnie White. "Seven Traits Separate KM Contenders & Pretenders." *KMWorld* 07.05 (27 April 2000): 36-37.

Murray, P. "How Smarter Companies Get Results from KM." *The Financial Times* (08 March 1999): 12-13.

Nakra, Prema. "Knowledge Management: The Magic Is in the Culture!" *Competitive Intelligence Review* 11.02 (Second Quarter 2000): 53-60.

Orlikowski, Wanda J. "Improvising Organizational Transformation Over Time: A Situated Change Perspective." *Information Systems Research: ISR: A Journal of the Institute of Management Sciences* 07.01 (1996): 63-92.

Orlikowski, Wanda J. "Learning from Notes: Organizational Issues in Groupware Implementation." *The Information Society* 09 (1993): 237-250.

Ostro, Nilly. "The Corporate Brain: Knowledge Management." *Chief Executive* 123 (May 1997): 58-62.

Papows, Jeff P. "The Payoff from Knowledge Management." *United States Banker* 109.09 (September 1999): 80.

Potter, David. "Go for 'Geek Speek'." *The Engineer* (11 June 1999): 10-11.

Prahalad, C. K. "Changes in the Competitive Battlefield." *The Financial Times* (04 October 1999): 01-04.

Prusak, L. "Making Knowledge Visible." *The Financial Times* (08 March 1999): 03.

Quinn, James Brian et al. "Managing Professional Intellect: Making the Most of the Best." *Harvard Business Review* (March-April 1996): 71.

Quintas, Paul et al. "Knowledge Management: A Strategic Agenda." *Long Range Planning* 30.03 (June 1997): 385-391.

Rolland, Colette et al. "Enterprise Knowledge Development: The Process View." *Information Management* 36.03 (September 1999): 165-184.

Saidel, Barbara and Don Cohen. "Case Study: Colaboration at Russell Reynolds Associates: The Power of Social Capital." IBM Institute for Knowledge Management, February 2000.

Samitt, Mindy K. "Knowledge Management in a Corporate Environment: An Annotated Bibliography." *Business & Finance Division Bulletin* (Winter 1999): 39-50.

Sanchez, Ron and Joseph T. Mahoney. "Modularity, Flexibility, and Knowledge Management in Product and Organization Design." *Strategic Management Journal* 17 (Winter 1996): 63-76.

Sauer, Steven D. "Managing Corporate Knowledge Can Yield Significant Dividends." *Healthcare Financial Management* 50.12 (December 1996): 31-32.

Schrage, Michael. "Thanks So Much For Your Advice; Now, Please Shut Up." *Fortune* 140.10 (22 November 1999): 372.

Schrage, Michael. "Why No One Wants Knowledge Management." *Computerworld* (07 December 1998).

Schwartz, Jeffrey. "Collaboration: More Hype Than Reality. True Knowledge Management Remains the Province of an Intrepid Few Organizations That Share Their Best Practices." *InternetWeek* 786 (25 October 1999): 64-66.

Siemers, Richard J. "KM: What's in It for Your Firm?" *American Banker* 165.29 (11 February 2000): 06.

Skyrme, David J. "Knowledge Management: Making It Work." *Law Librarian* 31.02 (June 1999): 84-90.

Smith, Linda C. "Track I: Knowledge Discovery, Capture and Creation." *Bulletin of the American Society for Information Science* 26.02 (December 1999-January 2000): 11-12.

"Special Issue: Knowledge and the Firm." *California Management Review* 40.03 (Spring 1998).

"Special Issue: Mastering Strategy." *The Financial Times* (04 October 1999).

Stamps, David. "A Conversation with Doctor Paradox." *Training* 34.05 (May 1997): 42-48.

Stamps, David. "Is Knowledge Management a Fad?" *Training* 36.03 (March 1999): 36-41.

Stauffer, David. "Why People Hoard Knowledge: To Get Them to Share It, You've Got to Overcome a Lot of History." *Across the Board* 36.08 (September 1999): 16-21.

Stear, Edward. "Ten Ways to Gain Management Support for Key Projects." *Online* 21.03 (May-June 1997): 103-104.

Stear, Edward B. "The Content Management Strategy: Don't Go to Work without It." *Online* 22.03 (May-June 1998): 87-90.

Stephenson, Carol. "How Carriers Can Become More Organizationally Nimble: A Case Study in Knowledge Creation." *Telecommunications* 31.08 (August 1997): 50-52.

Stewart, Thomas A. "Does Anyone Around Here Know...?" *Fortune* (29 September 1997).

Stewart, Thomas A. "Getting Real About Brainpower." *Fortune* 132.11 (27 November 1995): 201-203.

Stewart, Thomas A. "The Leading Edge: Time to Look at How You Manage Brainpower." *Fortune* 135 (23 June 1997): 159-161.

Stewart, Thomas A. "Packaging What You Know." *Fortune* (09 November 1998): 253.

Stewart, Thomas A. "Why Dumb Things Happen to Smart Companies." *Fortune* (23 June 1997).

Storer, Gary and Cheryl Harris. "Leap of Faith." *People Management* 05.07 (08 April 1999): 58-61.

Talukder, Majharul Islam. "Virtual Organization: Organization in the New Millennium." *Information Development* 15.04 (December 1999): 236-240.

Tapscott, Don. "Make Knowledge an Asset for the Whole Company." *Computerworld* (21 December 1998): 29.

Tolen, Franz A. L. "Knowledge Management: A Practical Approach." *Information Services and Use* 19.01 (1999): 57-61.

Tucker, Mark. "Who Owns the Customer?" *KMWorld* 07.11 (October 1998): 14.

Turner, Mary Johnston. "Knowledge Management Works When Everyone's Involved." *InternetWeek* (27 July 1998): 29.

Turoff, R. "An Arranged Marriage: Knowledge Management and Organizational Development." *American Programmer* 11.03 (March 1998): 30-33.

Tye, Carl. "Knowledge Management and Risk Management: Creating the Balance of Power." *KMWorld* 06.15 (20 October 1997): 50-53.

Tynan, Susan A. "Best Behaviors." *Management Review* 88.10 (November 1999): 58-61.

Velker, Lee. "Blending KM Technology with Culture." *KMWorld* 07.05 (27 April 1998): 10, 11, 60.

Walsh, J. P. and G. R. Ungston. "Organizational Memory." *Academy of Management Review* 16 (1991): 57-91.

Ward, Sandra. "Exchange Is No Robbery." *Journal of Information Science* 25.02 (March-April 1999): 157-163.

Watson, James and Joe Fenner. "The Role of Information Retrieval in Knowledge Management." *KMWorld* 07.06 (11 May 2000): 28, 30.

Watt, Peggy. "Knowing It All." *Network World* 14.33 (18 August 1997): 17-18.

Weick, K. "Prepare Your Organization to Fight Fires." *Harvard Business Review* 74.03 (1996): 143-148.

Wielinga, B. et al. "Methods and Techniques for Knowledge Management: What Has Knowledge Engineering to Offer?" *Expert Systems with Applications* 13.01 (July 1997): 73-84.

Wilson, Larry Todd and Diane Asay. "Putting Quality in Knowledge Management." *Quality Progress* 32.01 (January 1999): 25-31.

Wilson, O. "Knowledge Management: Putting a Good Idea to Work." *Managing Information* 05.03 (March 1998): 31-33.

Zack, Michael H. "Developing a Knowledge Strategy." *California Management Review* 41.03 (Spring 1999): 125-126.

Zemke, Ron and Susan. "Putting Competencies to Work." *Training* 36.01 (January 1999): 70-72.

KNOWLEDGE MANAGEMENT AND THE INFORMATION PROFESSIONAL

Information Technology is not the end-all, be-all of a Knowledge Management program. No matter how sophisticated a system is, it is created, maintained, and modified by human Information Professionals. Information Technology enables changes to occur within the organization. It does not make the changes in and of itself. That is the role of the employees and the Information Professionals. The Information Professional is able to assess current (and future) situations, determine the value of the technology that is in place, and make recommendations on the modifications that should occur. No machine can do that. No machine is yet able to reason.

The Human Capital of an organization is still its greatest asset. Knowledge Management enables an organization to create an environment that is conducive to making the greatest use of this asset. The Information Professional is the individual who is best educated and best prepared to take this untapped resource, add it to Information Technology that exists and utilize it to its greatest advantage, helping both the organization and the people within the organization. The Information Professional understands the technology, the people, and the processes that are a Knowledge Management system.

CIO's, CKO's, Information Specialists, Knowledge Facilitators... Knowledge Management has created new jobs and new functions. Knowledge Management has also had a great influence on existing information-oriented jobs like Librarians and Computer Technicians. Not only do all of these individuals (both The Old Guard and The New Kids) need to work together in order to create this new World of Knowledge, but they also have to learn to integrate the many changes that have taken place and will continue to be taking place within the organization.

Knowledge Management is not the express domain of any of these positions individually. All of these functions have something to contribute—and it is imperative that an atmosphere of mutual cooperation be created and fostered by the organization in order to allow the potential that exists within any organization to be realized.

Ways that these individuals can work together to create a new organizational World of Knowledge is discussed in the following articles.

Abram, Stephen. "Post Information Age Positioning for Special Librarians: Is Knowledge Management the Answer?" *Information Outlook* 01.06 (June 1997): 18-25.

Albert, Judith. "Is Knowledge Management Really the Future for Information Professionals?" Srikantaiah, Kanti and Michael E. D. Koenig, eds. *Knowledge Management for the Information Professional.* Medford, NJ: Information Today, 1999.

Arnold, Stephen E. "The Future Role of the Information Professional." *The Electronic Library* 17.06 (December 1999): 373-375.

Backer, Thomas E. "Information Alchemy: Transforming Information through Knowledge Utilization." *Journal of the American Society for Information Science* 44.04 (May 1993): 217-221.

Baker, Marc. "The Knowledge People." *British Journal of Administrative Management* 19 (March-April 2000): 18-19.

Balcombe, Jean. "Getting out of the Box: The Role of the Information Professional in Knowledge Management." *Law Librarian* 31.02 (June 1999): 91-95.

"Best Practices." *Industry Week* 249.02 (24 January 2000): 47.

Blake, Monica. "Focus: Sipping at the Fountain of Knowledge." *Information World Review* 151 (October 1999): 27-28.

Boeri, R. J. and M. Hensel. "Special Librarians and Enterprise Knowledge Management." *EMedia Professional* 11.04 (April 1998): 36.

Bonner D. "Enter the Chief Knowledge Officer." *Training & Development* 54.02 (February 2000).

Bowes, R. "Expanding the Information Horizon. Alternative Careers for Information Professionals." *ASLIB Proceedings* 43.09 (September 1991): 271-275.

Bradley, Phil. "Virtual Libraries and Internet Searching." *Online & CD-ROM Review* 23.06 (December 1999): 353-356.

Broadbent, Marianne. "The Emerging Phenomenon of Knowledge Management." *Australian Library Journal* 46.01 (February 1997): 06-24.

Broadbent, Marianne. "The Phenomenon of Knowledge Management: What Does it Mean to the Library Profession?" *Information Outlook* 02.05 (May 1998): 23-36.

Burns, T. and Shahida Rashid. "The New World of Information Professionalism." *Information Outlook* 03.07 (July 1999): 25-29.

Callaway, Erin. "Mind Meld." *PC Week* 13.15 (15 April 1996): 15-16.

Cascio, Jamais. "The Firing Squads Are Coming." *PC/Computing* (December 1999): 91.

Cates, Jo A. "Managing a Knowledge Management Career Search." *Business and Finance Division Bulletin* 113 (Winter 2000): 17-21.

Chase, R. L. "Knowledge Navigators." *Information Outlook* 02.09 (September 1998): 17-26.

"The Chief Knowledge Officer—A New Career Path?" *Information Advisor Knowledge Management Supplement* 02.02 (June 1998): 01-03.

Choo, Chun Wei et al. "A Behavioral Model of Information Seeking on the Web—Preliminary Results of a Study of How Managers and IT Specialists Use the Web." http://donturn.fis.utoronto.ca/research/esp/asis98.html

Copeland, Lee. "Harvesting Your Knowledge—Getting to Know Your Friendly Chief Knowledge Officer May Be a Good Idea." *Computer Reseller News* (26 October 1998).

Corcoran, Mary and Rebecca Jones. "Chief Knowledge Officers? Perceptions, Pitfalls, & Potential." *Information Outlook* 01.06 (June 1997): 30-36.

Cronin, Blaise et al. "The Emergent Market for Information Professionals: Educational Opportunities and Implications." *Library Trends* 42.02 (Fall 1993): 257-276.

Date, Shruti. "Agencies Create CKO Posts to Get in the Know." *Government Computer News* 18.36 (08 November 1999): 01.

Davenport, T. H. "Knowledge Roles, the CKO and Beyond." *CIO* 09.12 (1996): 24-29.

Davenport, Tom. "Coming Soon: The CKO." *InformationWeek* 491 (05 September 1994): 95.

Dess, Gregory G. and Joseph C. Picken. "Changing Roles: Leadership in the 21st Century." *Organizational Dynamics* 28.03 (Winter 2000): 18-34.

DiMattia, Susan and Norman Oder. "Knowledge Management: Hope, Hype, or Harbinger?" *Library Journal* 122.15 (15 September 1997): 33-35.

Drotos, P. V. "From Online Specialist to Research Manager: Changing with the Times." *Online* 18.01 (1994): 54-58.

Dysart, J. I. and Tom Davenport. "Tom Davenport on Knowledge Management: Selected Quotes." *Information Outlook* 01.06 (June 1997): 27-28.

Earl, M. J. and Ian A. Scott. "The Role of Chief Knowledge Officer." *The Financial Times* (08 March 1999): 05.

Earl, Michael J. and Ian A. Scott. "Opinion: What Is a Chief Knowledge Officer?" *Sloan Management Review* 40.02 (Winter 1999): 29-38.

Eddison, Betty and Susanne Bjorner. "Our Profession Is Changing: Whether We Like It or Not." *Online* 21.01 (January-February 1997): 72-81.

Edgar, S. "Knowledge Management: Has It Changed My Working Life? Will It Change Yours?" *Business Information Review* 16.03 (September 1999): 122-127.

Emerson, Toni. "What Comes After Knowledge Management? Wearable Computers, Smart Rooms, and Virtual Humans." *Information Outlook* 03.04 (April 1999): 13-14.

Empson, L. "The Challenge of Managing Knowledge." *The Financial Times* (04 October 1999): 08-10.

Field, Judith J. "Excellence and SLA." *Information Outlook* 02.03 (March 1998): 05.

Field, Judith J. "A New Year, New Challenges, and New Opportunities." *Information Outlook* 02.01 (January 1998): 05.

Fisher, A. "So What Is the Big Fuss About?" *Library Association Record* 100.04 (April 1998): 190-191.

Fitzsimmons, Gerard. "It's People Who Manage Knowledge—Not Computers!" *British Journal of Administrative Management* 19 (March-April 2000): 16.

Frisse, Mark E. et al. "Informatics and Medical Libraries: Changing Needs and Changing Roles." *Academic Medicine* 70.01 (January 1995): 30-35.

Fryer, Bronwyn. "Consulting's Next Big Thing." *Computerworld* 34.01 (03 January 2000): 94-95.

Funke, Susan. "In-House Content Providers: A New Role for Information Professionals." *Searcher: The Magazine for Database Professionals* 06.05 (May 1998): 45-47.

Ghilardi, Fiona J. Mellor. "The Information Center of the Future? The Professional's Role." *Online* 18 (November-December 1994): 08-09.

Gifford, Bernard R. "Where Is the Knowledge? Knowledge Management, Research and Pedagogy in the Electronic Age." *Education Libraries* 16.03 (Fall-Winter 1992): 14-22.

Goodfellow, Steve. "Who Is the Real MIS Manager in a Company Anyhow?" *KMWorld* 06.15 (20 October 1999): 24, 49.

Gustitus, Cheryl. "The Push Is on: What Push Technology Means to the Special Librarian." *Information Outlook* 02.01 (January 1998): 21-24.

Hale, David P. et al. "Business-IS Professional Differences: Bridging the Business Rule Gap." *Information Resources Management Journal* 12.02 (01 April 1999): 16.

Helfer, Joe. "A Practitioner's Guide to Knowledge Management." *Searcher: The Magazine for Database Professionals* 06.07 (01 July 1998): 44.

Herschel, Richard T. "Chief Knowledge Officer: Critical Success Factors for Knowledge Management." *Information Strategy: The Executive's Journal* 16.04 (Summer 2000): 37-45.

Hibbard, Justin. "Knowledge and Learning Officers Find Big Paydays." *InformationWeek* (15 June 1998): 170.

Jacso, Peter. "Savvy Searching." *Online & CD-ROM Review* 23.06 (December 1999): 345-348.

Jurek, Richard J. "An Argument for Change." *Marketing Research* 09 (Winter 1997): 56.

Keiser, Barbie E. "Justifying the Search and the Searcher." *Database Searcher* 08.06 (June 1992): 19-21.

Kennedy, Mary Lee. "Positioning Strategic Information: Partnering for the Information Advantage." *Special Libraries* 87.02 (Spring 1996): 120-131.

"KM in the Corporate Culture: CKO's Report." *KMWorld* 08.01 (January 1999): 20-21.

"Knowledge Management: Lessons for Information Professionals." *Information Advisor Knowledge Management Supplement* 01.01 (March 1997).

"Knowledge Management: The Third 'Era' of the Information Age." *InfoManage* 03.10 (September 1996): 01-05.

"Knowledge Workers." *Executive Excellence* 17.01 (January 2000): 15-16.

"Lack of Knowledge Management Leads to Skills Mismatch." *People Management* 06.07 (30 March 2000): 08.

"Leading HR Experts to Explore Technology's Effect on Managing People." *PR Newswire* 9513 (01 February 2000).

Lemon, Nancy. "Climbing the Value Chain: A Case Study in Rethinking the Corporate Library Function." *Online* 20.06 (November-December 1996): 50-56.

"Leveraging Knowledge Workers in the New Economy: Building Expert Directories to Increase Corporate Value." *Business Wire* 1456 (29 February 2000).

Lyon, Jo. "Personal Development—Understanding Knowledge." *Information World Review* 125 (May 1997): 24-25.

Mackenzie, Owen J. "Knowledge Management and the Information Professional." *Information Services & Use* 19.01 (1999): 07.

Marfleet, Jackie and Catherine Kelly. "Leading the Field: The Role of the Information Professional in the Next Century." *The Electronic Library* 17.06 (December 1999): 359-364.

Marshall, Lucy. "Facilitating Knowledge Management and Knowledge Sharing: New Opportunities for Information Professionals." *Online* 21.05 (September-October 1997): 92-98.

McClure, Charles R. and John C. Bertot. "The Chief Information Officer (CIO): Assessing Its Impact." *Government Information Quarterly* 17.01 (2000): 07-12.

Mills, Peter K. and Dan S. Moshavi. "Professional Concern: Managing Knowledge-Based Service Relationships." *International Journal of the Service Industry* 10.01 (1999): 48.

Murphy, Chris. "Reinventing the CIO: Tomorrow's IT Leaders Will Have to Be Part General, Part Maestro, and Part Evangelist." *InformationWeek* (10 January 2000): 48-62.

Nelke, M. "The Role of the Corporate Library in the Knowledge Management Process." *Information Services & Use* 19.01: 49-54.

Oxbrow, Nigel and Angela Abell. "Knowledge Environments: Where Are the Information Professionals?" *Business & Finance Division Bulletin* 112 (Fall 1999): 29-36.

Pearson, Pauline and Kevin Jones. "Developing Professional Knowledge: Making Primary Care Education and Research More Relevant. (Primary Care: Opportunities and Threats, Part 6)" *British Medical Journal* (1997): 817-820.

Pedley, P. "The Best Placed Profession to Give Tips on Filtering." *Library Association Record* 100.02 (February 1998): 82-83.

Pemberton, J. Michael. "Chief Knowledge Officer: The Climax of Your Career?" *Records Management Quarterly* 31.02 (April 1997): 66-69.

Peters, R. F. "Information Partnerships: Marketing Opportunities for Information Professionals." *Information Outlook* 01.03 (March 1997): 14-16.

Pigott, S. "New Roles for the Information Professional." *SLA Specialist* 19.09 (September 1996): 08.

Prusak, Laurence. "Hiring Outside the Box." *CIO* 08.18 (July 1995): 98.

Rowley, J. E. "Owners of the Knowledge." *Library Association Record* 101.08 (August 1999): 475.

Saunders, Laverna. "The Human Element in the Virtual Library." *Library Trends* 47-04 (Spring 1999): 771-787.

Schwartzwalder, Robert. "Librarians as Knowledge Management Agents." *EContent* 22.04 (August-September 1999): 63-65.

Schwartzwalder, Robert. "Manifesto: Seizing the Initiative in the Information Economy." *EContent* 23.01 (February-March 2000): 60-63.

Shein, Esther. "Balancing Act. (Women in IT)" *PC Week* 14.42 (06 October 1997): 111-114.

Sheridan, Elizabeth. "IH&RA: Remember the Human Element." *Hotel & Motel Management* 214.20 (15 November 1999): 03, 22.

Siegel, Gary. "Changing Work Roles Demand New Knowledge and Skills." *Strategic Finance* 81.08 (February 2000): 65-66.

Smith, Laura B. "The Thinkers." *PC Week* 13.31 (05 August 1996): E01-E02.

Solomon, Marc. "Re-Tooling the Information Professional." *Searcher: The Magazine for Database Professionals* 05.03 (March 1997): 10-14.

Solomon, Paul. "Discovering Information Behavior in Sense Making: III. The Person." http://ils.unc.edu/~solomon/person.html

St. Clair, G. "Knowledge Management for OPLs? Why Not?" *One-Person Library* 14.09 (January 1998): 01-02.

St. Clair, G. "Special Libraries." Line, Maurice et al, eds. *Library and Information Work Worldwide 1998*. London: Bowker-Saur, 1998.

St. Clair, G. and L. Remeikis. "Knowledge Management: The Third 'Era' of the Information Age?" *Records Management Bulletin* 77 (December 1996): 13-16.

Stear, E. B. and J. Wecksell. "Information Resource Center Management (IRCM)." *Bulletin of the American Society for Information Science* 23.04 (April-May 1997): 15-17.

Steele, Noreen O. "Corporate Makeover." *Library Journal* 122 (01 March 1997): 38-41.

Stewart, Thomas A. "Is This Job Really Necessary? Chief Knowledge Officers." *Fortune* 137.01 (12 January 1998): 154-155.

Stewart, Thomas A. "Smart Managing." *Fortune* 137 (12 January 1998): 154-155.

Stoker, David. "Wanted: An Innovative and Visionary Evidence-Based/Knowledge Management Librarian." *Journal of Librarianship & Information Science* 31.02 (June 1999): 67-69.

Stratigos, Anthea. "Choose Your Future." *Online* 24.01 (January-February 2000): 64-66.

Stricker, Ulla de. "Librarian 2000: A Personal Reflection on a Profession on the Verge." *Searcher: The Magazine for Database Professionals* 08.01 (January 2000): 124.

Strugatch, Warren. "Information Professionals Angst in the Information Age." *LI Business News* 47.05 (04 February 2000): 01A.

Taylor, V. "SLA Institute Focuses on Knowledge Management: A New Competitive Asset." *Library Hi Tech News* 150 (March 1998): 01-02.

Taylor, V. "Transform Yourself into a Knowledge Executive." *Information Outlook* 02.03 (March 1998): 16.

Tovstiga, George. "Profiling the Knowledge Worker in the Knowledge-Intensive Organization: Emerging Roles." *International Journal of Technology Management* 18.05, 06, 07, 08 (1999): 731-744.

Van Heust, G. et al. "Corporate Memories as a Tool for Knowledge Management." *Expert Systems with Applications* 13.01 (July 1997): 41-54.

Webber, Sheila. "Competencies for Information Professionals." *Bulletin of the American Society for Information Science* 26.01 (October-November 1999): 28-29.

Weinberger, David. "Three Days to a Smart Company." *KMWorld* 09.05 (June 2000): 16-17.

Weinberger, David. "You Want Knowledge? Hire a Teacher." *KMWorld* 07.12 (November 1998): 25.

Weinstein, Bob. "Knowledge Engineers in Demand." *Chicago Sun Times* (November 07, 1999): C01.

Williams, Ruth L. and Wendi R. Bukowitz. "Knowledge Managers Guide Information Seekers." *HR Magazine* 42 (January 1997): 76-81.

Wilson, Patrick. "Interdisciplinary Research and Information Overload." *Library Trends* 45.02 (Fall 1996): 192-203.

Wleklinski, Joann. "Leaving the Library: An Information Professional's Odyssey." *Searcher: The Magazine for Database Professionals* 05.07 (July 1997): 06-10.

Wleklinski, Joann. "Re-Tooling the Information Professional." *Searcher: The Magazine for Database Professionals* 05.07 (July-August 1997): 06-08.

Yerbury, Hilary. "Lost Ideas, Lost Cultures: Librarians in the Research Libraries in the 21st Century." *Information Development* 15.03 (September 1999): 155-159.

Zipperer, Lorri. "Librarians in Evolving Corporate Roles." *Information Outlook* 02.06 (June 1998): 27-30.

KNOWLEDGE MANAGEMENT ISSUES

Knowledge Management is thought by some to be a self-contained, individual department within the firm. Yes, the function it serves affects the firm in a direct manner—just as the Finance Department, the Marketing Department, etc. In fact, Knowledge Management is a truly inter-departmental function, providing all groups within the organization the opportunity to connect with one another and share valuable information.

Authority, cooperation, resource sharing, technology implementation, and territory...all of these issues are crucial to the executive whose responsibility includes the management of a department. In order to perform effectively, each group of employees must have the tools that enable them to perform their jobs well. Individuals involved with Knowledge Management are no different. As the newest addition to organizational culture, Knowledge Management must establish itself as a viable, contributing part of the organization. If Knowledge Management is perceived as simply another management fad that will fade into obscurity in six months, then it will never be given the opportunity or the resources that would allow it to succeed.

Besides the usual corporate in-fighting, there are other issues that Knowledge Management as a new discipline must face. These include the creation and maintenance of an atmosphere of trust and reciprocity within the firm, the creation of a knowledge-sharing environment, and the ethics of information and knowledge sharing and use, among others.

Becoming an accepted part of an organization is a difficult task, but it is even more difficult when no one in the organization knows how to measure the contribution. The creation of legitimacy for the work that Knowledge Management does, how to be taken seriously, how to get adequate financial and organizational support, how to get the organization actively involved in Knowledge Management...these are the first barriers a new Knowledge Management program faces, but they are certainly not the last. Advice on how to succeed in these difficult endeavors is given in the articles that follow.

Abrahams, Geraldine. "Climbing up the Lattice of Success." *CA Magazine* (October 1999): 81.

Adam, Lishan. "Web Content for Africa." *Information Development* 15.02 (June 1999): 127-132.

Adler, Paul S. "When Knowledge Is the Critical Resource, Knowledge Management Is the Critical Task." *IEEE Transactions on Engineering Management* 36.02 (May 1989): 87-94.

Aghion, Philippe and Patrick Bolton. "A Theory of Trickle-Down Growth and Development." *Review of Economic Studies* 64.02 (1997): 151-172.

Alavi, Maryam et al. "Knowledge Management Systems: Issues, Challenges, and Benefits." *Communications of the Association for Information Systems* (February 1999).

Albert, S. "Knowledge Management: Living up to the Hype?" *Midrange Systems* 11.13 (07 September 1998): 52.

Banerjee, Abhijit. "Simple Model of Herd Behavior." *Quarterly Journal of Economics* 107.03 (1992): 797-817.

Banks, Eric. "Creating a Knowledge Culture." *Work Study* 48.01 (04 March 1999): 18.

Barron, Daniel D. "The Digital Divide: Can School Librarians Help Build the Bridge?" *School Media Activities Monthly* 16.08 (April 2000): 47-51.

Barucci, Emilio. "Differential Games with Nonconvexities and Positive Spillovers." *European Journal of Operational Research* 121.01 (15 February 2000): 193-204.

Beghtol, C. "Knowledge Domains: Multidisciplinarity and Bibliographic Classification Systems." *Knowledge Organization* 25.01, 02 (1998): 01-12.

Berry, John N. "Bridge All the Digital Divides." *Library Journal* 125.09 (15 May 2000): 06.

Bolita, Dan. "HR Applications Target a Broader Audience." *KMWorld* 08.04 (April 1999): 58, 60.

Bolita, Dan. "Tom's of Maine and Beyond." *KMWorld* 09.01 (2000): 10-11.

Branscomb, Anne W. "Who Really Owns Public Information?" www.sis.pitt.edu/~slishtml/deans/lecture.html

Bresman, Henrik et al. "Knowledge Transfer in International Acquisitions." *Journal of International Business Studies* 30.03 (Third Quarter 1999): 439-462.

Brown, C. and S. Migill. "Alignment of the IS Functions with the Enterprise: Toward a Model of Antecedents." *Management Information Science Quarterly* 18.04 (1994): 371-403.

Burlton, R. "Process and Knowledge Management: A Question of Balance." *American Programmer* 11.03 (March 1998): 16-25.

Chuck, Lysabeth B. "Report from the Field. Simba's Online Publishing Conference: Industry Leaders Gathered in Florida to Discuss Product, Price and Promotion Strategies for the Online Business Market, and Touched on Issues Such as Content, Technologies, Channel Conflict, Knowledge Management, and Vertical Markets." *Information Today* 16.04 (1999): 22.

Cleveland, Harlan. "The Global Century." *Futures* 31.09-10 (November-December 1999): 887-895.

CommerceNet Research Center. "Search Engines Most Popular Method of Surfing the Web." http://www.commercenet.com

Creth, Sheila D. "Creating a Virtual Information Organization: Collaborative Relationships between Libraries and Computing Centers." *Journal of Library Administration* 19.03-04 (1993): 111-132.

Cropley, J. "Knowledge Management: A Dilemma." *Business Information Review* 15.01 (March 1998): 27-34.

Davenport, Tom. "Knowledge Management, Round Two." *CIO* 13.04 (01 November 1999): 30, 32-33.

Davenport, Tom. "Known Evils: Seven Fallacies That Can Hamper Development of Knowledge Management in a Company." *CIO* 10 (15 June 1997): 34-36.

Davenport, Tom. "Managing Customer Knowledge." *CIO* 11 (01 June 1998): 32-34.

Davenport, Tom. "Think Tank." *CIO* 08 (15 December 1995): 30-32.

Dickeson, Roger V. "Understanding Knowledge Workers." *Printing Impressions* 42.06 (November 1999): 76.

Dove, Rick. "Building a Principle-Based Knowledge Management Practice." *Automotive Manufacturing and Production* 110.02 (February 1998): 16-17.

Dove, Rick. "Knowledge Management—It's Not Just in the IT Department." *Automotive Manufacturing and Production* 110.03 (March 1998): 26-28.

Duberman, Josh and Michael Beaudet. "Privacy Perspectives for Online Searchers." *Searcher: The Magazine for Database Professionals* 08.07 (July-August 2000): 32-48.

Due, R. T. "The Eye of the Beholder: A Third Approach to Knowledge Management." *American Programmer* 11.03 (March 1998): 26-29.

Duffy, Jan. "Knowledge Management: To Be or Not to Be?" *Information Management Journal* 34.01 (January 2000): 64-67.

Essers, J. and J. Schreinemakers. "Nonaka's Subjectivist Conception of Knowledge in Corporate Knowledge Management." *Knowledge Organization* 24.01 (1997): 24-32.

"Executive Roundtable." *InformationWeek* (23 March 1998): 08ER-10ER.

Fahey, Liam and Laurence Prusak. "The Eleven Deadliest Sins of Knowledge Management." *California Management Review* 40.03 (Spring 1998): 265-276.

Fasoranti, Del. "Data Isn't Knowledge." *Cabinet Maker* 5182 (07 April 2000): 06.

Galagan, Patricia A. "Smart Companies." *Training & Development* 51.12 (December 1997): 20-24.

Gardner, Dana. "Get Smart: An Immature Knowledge Management Industry Tries to Overcome Content Chaos." *InfoWorld* 20.14 (06 April 1998): 97-98.

Ghilardi, Fiona J. Mellor. "Getting to 'Real-Time' Knowledge Management: From Knowledge Management to Knowledge Generation." *Online* 21 (September-October 1997): 99-100.

Ghoshal, Sumantra. "Changing the Role of Top Management: Beyond Structure to Processes." *Harvard Business Review* (January-February 1995): 86-91.

Gould, David M. and William C. Gruben. "The Role of Intellectual Property Rights in Economic Growth." *Journal of Development Economics* 48.03 (1996): 328-350.

Graham, Ann B. and Vincent G. Pizzo. "A Question of Balance: Case Studies in Strategic Knowledge Management." *European Management Journal* 14.04 (August 1996): 338-346.

Greif, Avner. "Cultural Beliefs and the Organization of Society: A Historical and Theoretical Reflection on Collectivist and Individualist Societies." *Journal of Political Economy* 102.05 (1994): 912-950.

Grenier, Ray and George Metes. "Wake up and Smell the Syzygy." *Business Communications Review* 28.08 (August 1998): 57-60.

"Harnessing Corporate IQ." *CA Magazine* 130 (April 1997): 26-29.

Hjalager, Anne-Mette. "Interorganizational Learning Systems." *Human Systems Management* 18.01 (01 January 1999): 23-32.

Hock, Ran. "How to Do Field Searching in Web Search Engines." *Online* 22.03 (1998): 18-22.

Hope, Kerin. "Albania Has Only 1.4 Fixed-Wire Telephones for Every 100 Inhabitants." *The Financial Times* (19 February 1997).

Hubbard, Elva Ellen. "KM, DM and Workflow Solutions Meet the Compliance Challenge." *KMWorld* 07.12 (November 1998): 26.

Hunter, R. "KM in Government: This is Not the Consulting Industry." *Research Note KM: KA 03-6492*. Stamford, CT: Gartner Group, 1998.

Hyden, Steven D. et al. "Identifying, Protecting, and Valuing Intellectual Property." *Journal of Asset Protection* 03.06 (July-August 1998): 32-38.

Intner, Sheila S. "The Good Professional: A New Vision." *American Libraries* 29.03 (March 1998): 48-50.

Ivers, Jack. "Presenting the Case for Automated Classification." *KMWorld* 08.04 (April 1999): 18.

Johannessen, Jon-Arild et al. "How Can Europe Compete in the 21st Century?" *International Journal of Information Management* 19.04 (August 1999): 263-275.

Jones, M. "Knowledge Management Column." *SIGGROUP Bulletin* 18.02 (August 1997): 16-18.

Jordan, Judith and Penelope Jones. "Assessing Your Company's Knowledge Management Style." *Long Range Planning* 30.03 (June 1997): 392-398.

Kaplan, R. S. and D. P. Norton. "The Balanced Score Card: Measures that Drive Performance." *Harvard Business Review* 70 (January-February 1992): 71-91.

Kerssens-Van Drongelen Inge C. et al. "Describing the Issues of Knowledge Management in R&D: Towards a Communication and Analysis Tool." *R&D Management* 26.03 (July 1996): 213-230.

Kinsella, William J. "Discourse, Power, and Knowledge in the Management of "Big Science"." *Management Communication Quarterly* 13.02 (November 1999): 171-208.

Knapp, Ellen. "Know-How's Not Easy: How to Keep Knowledge Management from Flickering Out." *Computerworld* 03.11 (17 March 1997): L01-L11.

"Know Thyself." *Industry Week* 249.02 (24 January 2000): 08.

"Knowledge Management: Fighting the Fad." *Online and CD-ROM Review* 22.02 (April 1998): 107-113.

Laberis, Bill. "One Big Pile of Knowledge." *Computerworld* 32.05 (02 February 1998): 97.

Lancaster, F. Wilfrid. "Second Thoughts on the Paperless Society: Technology Cannot Replace an Ethic of Public Service." *Library Journal* 124.15 (15 September 1999): 48-50.

Lawrence, Steve and C. Lee Giles. "Searching the World Wide Web." *Science* 280 (03 April 1998): 98-100.

Leadbeater, Charles. "Public Policy for the Knowledge Economy." *Knowledge Directions* 01 (Spring 1999): 72-81.

Lennon, David. "The Future of 'Free' Information on the Internet." *ASLIB Proceedings* 51.09 (October 1999): 285-289.

Levy, Steven and Brad Stone. "Hunting the Hackers." *Newsweek* (21 February 2000): 38-44.

Loucopolous, P. and V. Kavakli. "Enterprise Knowledge Management and Conceptual Modelling." *Lecture Notes in Computer Science* 1565 (1999): 123.

Maglitta, Joseph. "Smarten Up!" *Computerworld* 29.23 (05 June 1995): 84-86.

Malhotra, Y. "Knowledge Management and New Organization Forms a Framework for Business Model Innovation." *Information Resources Management Journal* 13.01 (January-March 2000): 05-14.

Malhotra, Yogesh. "Tools @ Work: Deciphering the Knowledge Management Hype." *Journal for Quality and Participation* 21.04 (July-August 1998): 58-60.

Malhotra, Yogesh. "Toward a Knowledge Ecology for Organizational White-Waters." http://brint.com/papers/ecology.htm

Marshall, Chris et al. "Financial Risk and the Need for Superior Knowledge Management." *California Management Review* 38.03 (Spring 1996): 77-101.

Martin, William J. "Approaches to the Measurement of the Impact of Knowledge Management Programmes." *Journal of Information Science* 26.01 (2000): 21-27.

Mazzie, Mark G. "Is Knowledge Management the Future of HR?" *KMWorld* 08.04 (April 1999): 58, 60.

McIntosh, Jennifer. "Leveraging Human Capital." *KMWorld* 08.04 (April 1999): 59-60.

Media Metrix. "Media Metrix Reports Top 25 Web Site and Web Property Rankings for April 1998." http://www.mediametrix.com

Milne, J. "Out One Ear, in the Other: Knowledge Management." *InformationWeek* (June 1998): 85-86.

Murray, Bill. "DOD Focuses on Knowledge Management but Can't Pin It Down." *Government Computer News* 19.04 (21 February 2000): 40.

Nerney, Chris. "Getting to Know Knowledge Management." *Network World* 14.39 (29 September 1997): 101.

Nerney, Chris. "Searching for True Knowledge." *Network World* 14.24 (16 June 1997): 42.

Nissen, Mark E. et al. "A Framework for Integrating Knowledge Process and System Design." *Information Strategy: The Executive's Journal* 16.04 (Summer 2000): 17-26.

Osin, Luis. "Computers in Education in Developing Countries: Why and How." *Education and Technology Series Paper No. 03(01)*. Washington, DC: Human Development Department Education Group—Education and Technology Team World Bank, 1998.

Oxbrow, Nigel. "Information Literacy: The Final Key to an Information Society." *Business and Finance Division Bulletin* 111 (Spring 1999): 39-41.

Prakash, A. et al. "Applications of Knowledge and Data Engineering: Data Management Issues and Trade-Offs in CSCW Systems." *IEEE Transactions on Knowledge and Data Engineering* 11.01 (1999): 213.

Prusak, Lawrence. "Laurence Prusak Shares Thoughts on Success and Knowledge Management." *Information Outlook* 03.05 (May 1999): 31-32.

Puccinelli, B. "Messaging Is the Medium." *Inform* 12.01 (January 1998): 24-27.

Riggs, F. W. "Onomantics and Terminology. Pt. I: Their Contributions to Knowledge Organization." *Knowledge Organization* 23.01 (1996): 25-30.

Riggs, Fred W. "Onomantics and Terminology. Pt. II: Core Concepts." *Knowledge Organization* 23.03 (1996): 157-168.

Safdie, Elias. "Integrating Autonomous Islands of Automation." *KMWorld* 07.04 (30 March 2000): 12, 14.

Sager, Ira et al. "Cyber Crime." *Business Week* (February 21, 2000): 36-42.

Sandberg, Jared. "Holes in the Net." *Newsweek* (21 February 2000): 47-49.

Schwartz, Karen D. "Feds Use the Internet and EDMS to Tackle Paper Glut." *KMWorld* 06.18 (01 December 1997): 30, 32.

Schwuchow, W. "Measuring the Information Market(s): A Personal Experience." *Journal of Information Science* 21.02 (1995): 123-132.

Silver, Bruce. "I Want My Rights!" *KMWorld* 09.05 (June 2000): 16-17.

Simonin, Bernard L. "Transfer of Marketing Know-How in International Strategic Alliances: An Empirical Investigation of the Role and Antecedents of Knowledge Ambiguity." *Journal of International Business Studies* 30.03 (Third Quarter 1999): 463-490.

Skyrme, David J. and Debra M. Amidon. "New Measures of Success." *Journal of Business Strategy* 19.01 (January 1998): 20-24.

Slater, Derek. "Knowledge Management: Do as I Say, Not as I Do." *CIO Enterprise* 11.04 (15 November 1997): 22.

Sly, Liz. "China's Trying to Cut off the Web." *Chicago Tribune* (27 January 1999): S01, S03.

Stamps, David. "Managing Corporate Smarts." *Training* 34 (August 1997): 40-44.

Stear, E. B. "Technology-Enabled Content: Threat or Opportunity." *Online* 21.04 (July-August 1997): 80-82.

Styffe, Elizabeth J. "Privacy, Confidentiality, and Security in Clinical Information Systems: Dilemmas and Opportunities for the Nurse Executive." *Nursing Administration Quarterly* 21.03 (1997): 21-28.

Teece, David. "Research Directions for Knowledge Management." *California Management Review* 40.03 (Spring 1998): 289-292.

Tsui, Eric. "Knowledge Management: Common Applications, Inadequacies and Educational Issues." http://murl.microsoft.com/LectureDetails.asp?518

"Unearthing Your Company's Hidden Knowledge: How to Create a Best Practice Identification System." *Business Wire* 1532 (01 February 2000).

van Mesdag, Martin. "Too Much Information, Not Enough Knowledge." *Chief Executive* (May 1983): 38-39.

Wagner, Cynthia G. and Jeff Minard. "On the Frontiers of Wisdom." *Futurist* 33.09: 51-56.

Ward, Patricia Layzell. "Information 2000: Has It Happened, or Is It Happening?" *Online and CDROM Review* 23.06 (December 1999): 349-351.

Willard, N. "Knowledge Management: What Does It Imply for IRM?" *Managing Information* 04.08 (October 1997): 31-32.

Zerega, Blaise. "Art of Knowledge Management: Experts Caution That Consultants' Methodologies May Vary Widely." *InfoWorld* 20.30 (27 July 1998): 61.

Zha, X. F. "Integrated Knowledge-Based Approach and System for Product Design for Assembly." *International Journal of Computer Integrated Manufacturing* 12.03 (01 May 1999): 211.

Zuckerman, Amy. "Are You Really Ready for Knowledge Management?" *Journal for Quality and Participation* 20.03 (June 1997): 58-61.

Zuckerman, Amy and Hal Buell. "Is the World Ready for Knowledge Management?" *Quality Progress* 31.06 (June 1998): 81-84.

KNOWLEDGE MANAGEMENT AND INFORMATION TECHNOLOGY

The Information Technology boom has benefited everyone—but few more so than those in the field of Knowledge Management. Knowledge Management has also assisted in the development of new Information Technology, as well. It is obvious that each of these areas is dependent upon the other to assist each other's respective growth. The technology that has been (and continues to be) developed has provided Knowledge Management the technological ability to fulfill its mission.

What Information Technology does is provide a platform, a foundation upon which to build a Knowledge Management program. Without Information Technology, those in the field of Knowledge Management could still perform their function, but I am certain that it would be far more difficult. Information Technology is one side of the triangle that is Knowledge Management. The other two include Information Professionals and Processes, both of which are discussed in other parts of this Bibliography.

While Information Technology is, in fact, an integral part of Knowledge Management, Information Technology is a Knowledge Management enabler—not the sum total of a Knowledge Management program. It is easy to get caught up in the desire to have state-of-the-art technology in one's firm, but it is imperative that an organization not stake its Knowledge Management program on the purchase of new computer products. The other two sides of the triangle must be accounted for as well.

Knowledge Management practitioners must never forget the human element and the processes that allow Information Technology to work. What follows is a selection of articles describing the value of Information Technology in the realm of Knowledge Management.

Abramson, Gary. "Operation Brain-Trap." *CIO Enterprise* 13.04 (15 November 1999): 78, 80, 82.

Abramson, Gary. "Wiring the Corporate Brain." *CIO* 12.11 (March 1999): 30-36.

Agada, John. "Repackaging Information." Srikantaiah, Kanti and Michael E. D. Koenig, eds. *Knowledge Management for the Information Professional.* Medford, NJ: Information Today, 1999.

Allerton, Haidee E. "Thing One and Thing Two." *Training & Development* 52 (February 1998): 09.

Alter, Allan E. "Know-How Pays Off." *Computerworld* 31.02 (13 January 1997): 72.

American Productivity and Quality Center. "Knowledge Management Consortium Benchmarking Study, Final Report." (1996).

American Productivity and Quality Center. "Using Information Technology to Support Knowledge Management, Final Report." (1997).

Amoroso, Alfred J. and Mary Ann Garwood. "Investing in Technology Is a Matter of Survival." *Best's Review* 96.08 (December 1995): 90-92.

Balasubramanian, P. et al. "Managing Process Knowledge for Decision Support." *Decision Support Systems* 27.01-02 (November 1999): 145-162.

Balisani, Ettore and Enrico Scarso. "Information Technology Management: A Knowledge-Based Perspective." *Technovation* 19.04 (01 April 1999): 209.

Balla, John et al. "Knowledge Management Comes of Age." *Inform* 13.07 (July 1999): 22-29.

Berry, John. "Real Knowledge Is Held by People." *InternetWeek* (10 January 2000): 31.

Berry, John et al. "Securing an Information Future." *Library Journal* 124.12 (July 1999): 54.

Biggs, Maggie. "Enterprise Toolbox: Resurgent Text-Mining Technology Can Greatly Increase Your Firm's 'Intelligence' Factor." *InfoWorld* 22.02 (10 January 2000): 52.

Black, Ken. "Internet Search Engines and Knowledge Management." Srikantaiah, Kanti and Michael E.D. Koenig, eds. *Knowledge Management for the Information Professional*. Medford, NJ: Information Today, 1999.

Blough, Kay. "In Search of More-Secure Extranets." *Informationweek* 759 (01 November 1999): 94-100.

Blumentritt, Rolf and Ron Johnston. "Towards a Strategy for Knowledge Management." *Technology Analysis & Strategic Management* 11.03 (September 1999): 287-300.

Boisot, M. and D. Griffiths. "Possession is Nine Tenths of the Law: Managing a Firm's Knowledge Base in a Regime of Weak Appropriability." *International Journal of Technology Management* 17.06: 662-676.

Bond, James. "The Drivers of the Information Revolution: Cost, Computing Power and Convergence." *The Information Revolution and the Future of Telecommunications*. Washington, DC: World Bank, 1997.

Bond, James. "How Information Infrastructure Is Changing the World." *The Information Revolution and the Future of Telecommunications*. Washington, DC: World Bank, 1997.

Bond, James. "Telecommunications Is Dead, Long Live Networking—The Effect of the Information Revolution on the Telecom Industry." *The Information Revolution and the Future of Telecommunications*. Washington, DC: World Bank, 1997.

Bookstein, Abraham. "Information Coding in the Internet Environment." Srikantaiah, Kanti and Michael E.D. Koenig, eds. *Knowledge Management for the Information Professional*. Medford, NJ: Information Today, 1999.

Bourdreau, A. and G. Couiliard. "Systems Integration and Knowledge Management." *Information Systems Management* 16.04 (Fall 1999): 24-32.

Boyd, S. "Operational Knowledge Management: Strategic Alignment and Enterprise Architecture." *Cutter IT Journal* 12.11 (November 1999): 27-31.

Braga, Carlos A. Primo. "Liberalizing Telecommunications and the Role of the World Trade Organization." *The Information Revolution and the Future of Telecommunications*. Washington, DC: World Bank, 1997.

Braga, Carlos A. Primo and Carsten Fink. "The Private Sector and the Internet." *The Information Revolution and the Future of Telecommunications*. Washington, DC: World Bank, 1997.

Brown, Donna W. "An Ambiguous Relationship with the Internet." *Book Report* 18.03 (November-December 1999): 38.

Burn, J. M. and C. Ash. "Knowledge Management Strategies for Virtual Organisations." *Information Resources Management Journal* 13.01 (January-March 2000): 15-23.

Carayannia, Elias G. "Fostering Synergies Between Information Technology and Managerial and Organizational Cognition: The Role of Knowledge Management." *Technovation* 19.04 (01 April 1999): 219.

Chatterji, Deb. "Strategic Impact of the Information Age." *Research Technology Management* 43.01 (January-February 2000): 35-37.

Chudnov, Daniel. "Open Source Software: The Future of Library Systems?" *Library Journal* 124.13 (August 1999): 40-43.

Clark, Patricia. "Disciplinary Structures on the Internet." *Library Trends* 45.02 (Fall 1996): 226-238.

Clippinger, John H. "Visualization of Knowledge: Building and Using Intangible Assets Digitally." *Planning Review* 23.06 (November-December 1995): 28-32.

Clottes, Francoise. "The Information Revolution and the Role of Government." *The Information Revolution and the Future of Telecommunications*. Washington, DC: World Bank, 1997.

Coleman, David. "Knowledge Management: The Next Golden Egg in Groupware." *Computer Reseller News* 729 (31 March 1997): 79-80.

"Confusing Terminology." *Computerworld* (10 January 2000): 68.

Copeland, Lee. "One-Stop Knowledge Shop." *Computerworld* 34.06 (07 February 2000): 74.

Counsell, J. et al. "Schemebuilder: Computer-Aided Knowledge-Based Design of Mechatronic Systems." *Assembly Automation* 19.02: 129-138.

Cox, E. "What Does Your Company Really Do? Data Fusion in the Era of Knowledge Management." *PC AI* 13.04 (July-August 1999): 37.

Crossley, M. et al. "The Knowledge Garden." *BT Technology Journal* 17.01: 76-84.

Cuena, J. and M. Molina. "The Role of Knowledge Modeling Techniques in Software Development: A General Approach Based on a Knowledge Management Tool." *International Journal of Human Computer Studies* 52.03 (01 March 2000): 385-421.

Currid, Cheryl. "The Business of Knowledge." *Web Techniques* 05.04 (April 2000): 24.

Darzentas, Jenny. "Sharing Metadata: Enabling Online Information Provision." *OCLC Systems and Services* 15 (04 November 1999): 172-178.

Davenport, Tom. "Saving IT's Soul: Human-Centered Information Management." *Harvard Business Review* (March-April 1994): 119-131.

David, P. A. "The Dynamo and the Computer: An Historical Perspective on the Modern Productivity Paradox." *American Economic Review* 80.02: 355-361.

Davidson, Clive. "The Corporate Brain Transplant." *New Statesman* 12.574 (27 September 1999): xii.

Dempsey, Larcan. "The Network and the Library: Working in a New Shared Space; Infrastructure and Institutions." *The Electronic Library* 17.04 (August 1999): 201-211.

Dieng, R. et al. "Methods and Tools for Corporate Knowledge Management." *International Journal of Human-Computer Studies* 51.03 (September 1999): 567-598.

DiRomualdo, Anthony and Vijay Gurbaxani. "Strategic Intent for IT Outsourcing." *Sloan Management Review* 39.04 (Summer 1998): 67-80.

"Document and Knowledge Management: After-Hype: KM Enters Critical 7 Phase." *Computing Canada* 26.08 (14 April 2000): 13.

Dooley, K. J. et al. "Process Knowledge Bases: Understanding Processes through Cause and Effect Thinking." *Human Systems Management* 17.04: 281-296.

Elam, Dan. "From Push Technology, New Applications Will Emerge." *KMWorld* 07.02 (23 February 1998): 17-21.

Feldman, Susan and Edmund Yu. "Intelligent Agents: A Primer." *Searcher: The Magazine for Database Professionals* 07.09 (October 1999): 42.

Fiddler, Ileen. "Knowledge Management and Vocabulary Control." Srikantaiah, Kanti and Michael E. D. Koenig, eds. *Knowledge Management for the Information Professional.* Medford, NJ: Information Today, 1999.

Field, Judy. "Extranets: A New Tool For Your Future." *Computers in Libraries* 19.01 (01 October 1998).

Finerty, Pat. "Improving Customer Care Through Knowledge Management." *CMA Magazine* 71.09 (November 1997): 33.

Fontana, John. "Lotus Knowledge Management Plan Takes Flight." *Network World* 16.44 (01 November 1999): 14.

Ford, Nigel. "From Information to Knowledge Management: The Role of Rule Induction and Neural Net Machine Learning Techniques in Knowledge Generation." *Journal of Information Science Principles and Practice* 15.04-05 (1989): 299-304.

Frappaolo, Carl. "What's in a Name?" *KMWorld* 07.03 (16 March 1998): 18-19.

Friedman, Sam. "Internet Explosion Is Risky Business." *National Underwriter* 103.17 (26 April 1999): 13.

Fu, Limin. "Knowledge Discovery Based on Neural Networks." *Communications of the ACM* 42.11 (November 1999): 47.

"FutureNext: Knowledge Management Expert Keynotes DCI's Data Warehouse World." *PR Newswire* 7834 (25 October 1999).

Gallivan, M. "Value in Triangulation: A Comparison of Two Approaches for Combining Quantitative and Qualitative Methods." Liebenau, Lee A. J. and J. De Gross, eds. *Qualitative Method in Information Systems*. New York: Chapman & Hall, 1997.

Gartner, Gideon. "Grappling with eKnowledge." *Computerworld* 32.01 (29 December 1997-05 January 1998): 43.

Gibson, Paul. "Knowledge Management Makes it Online: Publisher Web Sites Now Offer a Range of Long-Awaited KM Resources." *Information Today* 15.06 (June 1998): 46.

Glatzer, Hal. "Software Is the Key to Managing Knowledge." *KMWorld* 06.16 (17 November 1997): 20, 24.

Goodfellow, Steve. "Consolidating Administrative Duties." *KMWorld* 06.16 (17 November 1997): 28-29.

Goodfellow, Steve. "Tried (and Trendy) Ways to Secure Your Knowledge." *KMWorld* 07.12 (November 1998): 21-22.

Gough, C. "Appraising Your Knowledge Management Initiative." *Computers and Law* 10.03 (August-September 1999): 19-22.

Graves, William and Bud Sonka. "Moving the Network Revolution in Knowledge Management beyond Random Acts of Progress." *Serials Librarian* 38.01/02 (2000): 25-30.

Gray, Carol Lippert. "Heads Up: Here Comes Your Next IT Challenge." *Financial Executive* (May-June 1999): 22-23.

Gundry, John and George Metes. "Team Knowledge Management: A Computer-Mediated Approach." http://www.knowab.co.uk/wbwteam.html

Halpern, Marc. "Capitalizing on Knowledge-Based Engineering." *Computer-Aided Engineering* 19.02 (February 2000): 47.

Hauer, M. "Three Thousand Years of Knowledge Management: What Can We Learn from Science?" *Information Services & Use* 19.01: 37-44.

Heitor, Manuel and David Gibson. "Knowledge Transfer and Application: Key to Growth." *Research Technology Management* 42.01 (January-February 1999): 07-08.

Hendriks, P. H. J. "Do Smarter Systems Make for Smarter Organizations?" *Decision Support Systems* 27.01-02 (November 1999): 197-211.

Hendriks, Paul H. and Dirk J. Vriens. "Knowledge-Based Systems and Knowledge Management: Friends or Foes?" *Information & Management* 69.01 (February 1999): 113-125.

Holsapple, Clyde W. "Adapting Demons to Knowledge Management Environments." *Decision Support Systems* 03.04 (December 1987): 289-298.

Janes, Kathy. "KM—A Mental Clearing House for the Mind?" *DM Review* 09.10 (November 1999): 68-69.

Joachim, David and David Drucker. "Grand Vision, Tall Order: Customers Skeptical That Lotus Can Make Knowledge Management Work." *InternetWeek* (24 January 2000): 01.

Joachim, David and David Drucker. "Knowledge Management Work." *InternetWeek* (24 January 2000): 01.

Kellogg, C. "From Data Management to Knowledge Management." *Computer* 19.01 (January 1986): 75-84.

Kempster, Linda S. "Mass Storage: Future Trends and Applications." *KMWorld* 06.16 (17 November 1997): 16-19, 25-27.

Kennedy, M. L. "Building Blocks for Knowledge Management at Digital Equipment Corporation: The WebLibrary." *Information Outlook* 01.06 (June 1997): 39-48.

King, Julia. "Customer Reps Play Favorites: Software Clues Them in When Big Spenders Call." *Computerworld* (08 February 1999): 01.

King, Julia. "Knowledge Management Promotes Sharing." *Computerworld* 32.24 (15 June 1998): 24.

King, W. R. "Integrating Knowledge Management into IS Strategy." *Information Systems Management* 16.04 (Fall 1999): 70-72.

Klein, Mark. "Managing Knowledge Drives Key Decisions." *National Underwriter* 103.13 (29 March 1999): 31.

"KM Market Grows." *Computer Dealer News* 16.01 (07 January 2000): 20.

"Knowledge Equals Power." *InfoWorld* 19.46 (17 November 1997): 116-124.

Koenig, Michael E. D. "Data Relationships: Information Retrieval Systems and DataBase Management Systems (DBMS)." *Information Technology and Libraries* 04.03 (September 1985): 247-272.

Lamont, Judith. "Even-Handed XML Brings Commonality to Diverse Applications." *KMWorld* 09.05 (June 2000): 10-12.

LaPlante, Alice. "Sharing the Wisdom." *Computerworld* 31.22 (02 June 1997): 73-74.

LaSalle, Jones Lan. "The Digital Midas Touch." *Estates Gazette* (06 June 1999): 134-135.

Lattig, Michael. "Tacit Tapping E-Mail for Knowledge Sharing." *InfoWorld* 21.44 (01 November 1999).

Lee, Heeseok and Jae-Woo Joung. "An Enterprise Model Repository: Architecture and System." *Journal of Database Management* 11.01 (January-March 2000): 16-28.

Lewis, Bob. "IS Survival Guide: Don't Become an E-Head. Just Support Your Business Strategy with Technology." *InfoWorld* 22.08 (21 February 2000): 70.

Lewis, Ted. "Where the Smart Money Is?" *Computer* 32.11 (November 1999).

Lin, Herbert. "Fluency with Information Technology." *Government Information Quarterly* 17.01 (2000): 69-76.

Longbottom, Clive. "It's the Way You Use It." *Computing* (18 March 1999): 30.

"Lotus White Paper: Lotus, IBM, and Knowledge Management." (1998).

Luke, Michael O. "The Information Future." *Online* 20.01 (January-February 1996): 65-68.

Macht, Joshua. "Confessions of an Information Sinner." *Inc.* 21.01 (January 1999): 73-76.

"Making the Knowledge Economy Work for You: Best Practices for Knowledge Sharing Systems." *Business Wire* 1747 (23 February 2000).

Malcolm, Stanley E. "Where EPSS Will Go from Here." *Training* 35 (March 1998): 64-66.

Malloy, Amy. "You Have It Now." *Computerworld* 32.08 (23 February 1998): 78.

Manchester, P. "Tools for Knowledge Management." *The Financial Times* (08 March 1999): 11.

Mascitelli, R. "A Framework for Sustainable Advantage in Global High-Tech Markets." *International Journal of Technology Management* 17.03: 240-258.

Maurer, H. "Web-Based Knowledge Management." *Computer* 31.03 (March 1998): 122-123.

McCune, Jenny C. "Thirst for Knowledge." *Management Review* 88.04 (April 1999): 10-12.

McKenna, Brian Martin. "Humanware?" *Online & CD-ROM Review* 23.01 (February 1999): 43-47.

Mullin, Rick. "Knowledge Management: Hearts and Minds Connect On-Line." *Chemical Week* (19 January 2000): 28-29.

Musier, Reiner. "Knowledge Management, Integrated Process Software and Work Process Integration Will Drive Process Simulation and Plant Optimization." *Chemical Market Reporter* 257.13 (27 March 2000): 14-15.

"New Paper-to-Digital Solution from Adobe Unleashes Knowledge Trapped in Paper Documents." *PR Newswire* 8373 (31 January 2000).

Nissen, M. et al. "Integrated Analysis and Design of Knowledge Systems and Processes." *Information Resources Management Journal* 13.01 (January-March 2000): 24-43.

O'Leary, D. E. "Knowledge Management Systems: Converting and Connecting." *IEEE Intelligent Systems* (May-June 1998): 30-33.

Olin, Jack D. et al. "Knowledge Management across Multi-Tier Enterprises: The Promise of Intelligent Software in the Auto Industry." *European Management Journal* 17.04 (August 1999): 334-347.

Pan, Shan L. and Harry Scarbrough. "Knowledge Management in Practice: An Exploratory Case Study." *Technology Analysis & Strategic Management* 11.03 (September 1999): 359-374.

Pancerella, C. M. and N. M. Berry. "Adding Intelligent Agents to Existing EI Frameworks." *IEEE Internet Computing* 03.05 (September-October 1999): 60-61.

Pearson, Thomas A. "Measurements and the Knowledge Revolution." *Quality Progress* 32.09 (September 1999): 31-37.

Pemberton, Jeff and Thomas Pack. "The Cutting-Edge Library at Hewlett-Packard: Bringing Together Knowledge, Access, and Tools." *Online* 23.05 (September-October 1999): 30-34.

Perez, Ernest. "Knowledge Management in the Library: Not." *Database* 22.02 (April 1999): 75-78.

Petrovic, Otto et al. "Learning Aspects of Knowledge Management and New Technologies." *Journal of European Industrial Training* 22.07 (1998): 277-288.

Peuschel, P. et al. "A Knowledge-Based Software Development Environment Supporting Cooperative Work." *International Journal on Software Engineering and Knowledge Engineering* 02.01 (1992).

Preston, C. M. and C. A. Lynch. "Report of the First International Conference on Information and Knowledge Management." *Library Hi-Tech News* 102 (May 1993): 07-08.

Pukszta, Helen. "Forget Knowledge Management: Back to Information." *Computerworld* 33.18 (03 May 1999): 32.

Puzzanghera, P. "The Bigger Picture." *Intelligent Enterprise* 02.05 38-40, 42, 44.

Quint, Barbara. "Search Engine Designer for Tomorrow: Interview with TextWise's Elixabeth Liddy." *Searcher: The Magazine for Database Professionals* 06.03 (March 1998): 19-23.

Radding, Alan. "The Rush to XML—Technology Will Let Companies Interact More Easily on the Web." *InformationWeek* (03 January 2000).

Rischard, Jean-Francois. "Connecting Developing Countries to the Information Technology Revolution." *SAIS Review* 16 (Winter-Spring 1996): 93-107.

Russom, Philip. "New Directions for Knowledge Management Software." *DM Review* 09.09 (October 1999): 44-45, 49.

Sah, Raaj K. and Joseph E. Striglitz. "Sources of Technological Divergence between Developed and Less Developed Economies." Calvo, G. et al, eds. *Debt, Stabilization, and Development*. Baltimore, MD: Johns Hopkins University Press, 1993.

Sahasrabudhe, Vikas. "Information Technology in Support of Knowledge Management." Srikantaiah, Kanti and Michael E. D. Koenig, eds. *Knowledge Management for the Information Professional*. Medford, NJ: Information Today, 1999.

Sarel, Michael. "Growth in East Asia: What We Can and What We Cannot Infer." *Economic Issues No. 1*. Washington, DC: International Monetary Fund, 1997.

Sawyer, S. and R. Southwick. "Implementing Client-Server: Issues from the Field." Glasson, B. et al., eds. *The International Office of the Future*. New York: Chapman & Hall, 1996.

Scarbrough, Harry. "Systems Error." *People Management* 05.07 (08 April 1999): 68-72.

Schohl, W. and V. Vocke-Schohl. "A System for Universal Knowledge Management Using Online Hosts, the Internet and Internal Intranet-Databases." *NFD Information—Wissenschaft und Praxis* 50.06 (September 1999): 347-353.

Schroeder, Erica. "Searching for the Right Knowledge." *PC Week* 16.16 (19 April 1999): 68.

Schwartzwalder, Robert. "The Extraordinary Extranet." *EContent* 22.06 (December 1999): 70-72.

Seiler, H. "Knowledge Management and Microsoft's Active Platform2." *PC AI* 12.05: 27-30.

"Share the Knowledge. Knowledge-Management Apps Will Have to Be Integrated with Other Tools to Realize Their Full Potential." *InformationWeek* 752 (13 September 1999): 65.

Shen, Sheldon. "Knowledge Management in Decision Support Systems." *Decision Support Systems* 03.01 (March 1987): 01-11.

Sherman, Chris. "New Web Map Reveals Previously Unseen 'Bow-Tie' Organizational Structure." *Information Today* 17.07 (July-August 2000): 56.

Simon, E. and W. Bredemeier. "Electronic Information Services as an Instrument for Foreign Advantage." *NFD Information—Wissenschaft und Praxis* 50.03 (June 1999): 179-186.

Skyrme, D. J. "Knowledge Management Solutions: The IT Contribution." *SIGGROUP Bulletin* 19.01: 34-39.

Spencer, Harvey. "Capturing Explicit Knowledge." *KMWorld* 06.18 (01 December 1997): 18.

Steele, N. "United Technologies Corporation Moves to Virtual Information Services." *Bulletin of the American Society for Information Science* 24.06: 13-16.

Strapko, William. "Knowledge Management: A Fit with Expert Tools." *Software Magazine* 10.13 (November 1990): 63-66.

Strassmann, Paul A. "The Knowledge Fuss." *Computerworld* 33.40 (04 October 1999): 46.

Taft, Darryl K. "Stopping Knowledge Overflow: Knowledge Management Tools Still in Developmental Phase." *Computer Reseller News* (28 February 2000): 59.

Taylor, Volney. "Technology Innovation and Processing Information: Content and Context." *Vital Speeches of the Day* 65.07 (15 January 1999): 201-204.

Terveen, Loren G. et al. "Living Design Memory: Framework, Implementation, Lessons Learned." *Human-Computer Interaction* 10.01 (1995): 01-37.

"TFPL Survey of Knowledge Management Roles and Skills." *Program-Electronic Library and Information Systems* 34.01 (January 2000): 113-114.

Tidd, Ronald R. "Web Search Engines and Directories: The First Step in Knowledge Management." *Taxes* 77.10 (October 1999): 05-06.

Tolomen, Eva. "Facing Future Users: The Challenge of Transforming a Traditional Online Database into a Web Service." *OCLC Systems and Services* 15 (04 November 1999): 160-164.

Trembly, Ara C. "Managing Knowledge Takes More Than Tech." *National Underwriter (Property & Casualty/Risk & Benefits Management Edition)* 103.20 (17 May 1999): 47.

Tuomi, Ilkka. "Data Is More Than Knowledge: Implications of the Reversed Knowledge Hierarchy for Knowledge Management and Organizational Memory." *Journal of Management Information Systems: JMIS* 16.03 (1999): 103-118.

Turner, Mary Johnston. "Migrating to Network-Based Application Services." *Business Communications Review* 29.02 (February 1999): 48-51.

Tyler, G. "Well, What D'ya Know?" *Management Services* 43.06: 28-31.

Tyler, G. "How to Be a Know-All." *Management Accounting* 78.01 (January 2000): 32-34.

Ubois, Jeff. "From Web Sites to Knowledge Management." *Midrange Systems* 10.19 (28 November 1997): 24.

Vassallo, P. "The Knowledge Continuum: Organizing for Research and Scholarly Communication." *Internet Research: Electronic Networking Applications and Policy* 09.03: 232-242.

Violino, Bob. "Customer at the Core." *InformationWeek* (27 September 1999): 302-308.

"The Virtual Office: Groupware Creates Consultants' Office Without Walls." *San Francisco Business Times* 12.18 (19 December 1997): S06-S07.

Warner, Julian. "On Universality in Productive and Information Technology." *ASLIB Proceedings* 41.05 (May 1999): 167-171.

Watkins, Karen E. and Mary Wilson Callahan. "Return on Knowledge Assets: Rethinking Investments in Educational Technology." *Educational Technology* 38.04 (July-August 1998): 33-40.

Watson, Gregory H. "Bringing Quality to the Masses: The Miracle of Loaves and Fishes." *Quality Progress* 03.06 (June 1998): 29-32.

Weinberger, D. "Unmanaging Knowledge." *Cutter IT Journal* 12.11 (November 1999): 32-35.

Westbrook, Lynn. "Pinning the Shift: Examining the Impact of Information Technology on Personal and Institutional Roles." *The Journal of Academic Librarianship* 26.01 (January 2000): 59-63.

White, Curt M. "Telecommunications and Networks in Knowledge Management." Srikantaiah, Kanti and Michael E. D. Koenig, eds. *Knowledge Management for the Information Professional.* Medford, NJ: Information Today, 1999.

Wilck, Jennifer. "IT Drivers Are Myriad for Chemical Manufacturers." *Chemical Market Reporter* 251 (19 May 1997): 21.

Wilson, L. T. and C. A. Snyder. "Knowledge Management and IT: How Are They Related?" *IT Professional* 01.02: 73-75.

WorldSpace. "WorldSpace: The Technology." http://www.worldspace.com

Young, Kung. "Put All Your Eggs in One Basket." *Banker* 150.890 (April 2000): 104-105.

Zimmerman, Kim Ann. "Collaborative Computing: A Must for Government." *KMWorld* 07.04 (30 March 2000): 16-18.

Zoellick, Bill. "New Level of Integration or New Technology?" *KMWorld* 07.03 (16 March 2000): 32-33.

KNOWLEDGE MANAGEMENT AND INTRANETS

Information Technology, as stated earlier, has had a major impact on the evolution and development of Knowledge Management. One of the applications of Information Technology to evolve that has had a singularly potent effect on Knowledge Management is the Intranet—an internal network of connected work stations and servers whose purpose is to link related (or seemingly unrelated) functions and personnel in an effort to make Knowledge Sharing and Knowledge Management easier, faster, and more efficient.

The Intranet is a powerful tool, but it is just that—a tool. Regardless of its power, its potential, or its reach, Information Technology still has one shortfall—it cannot create knowledge. Information Technology provides a platform for it, stores it, and makes it accessible, but it cannot create it. The human element is still the over-riding factor that makes Knowledge Management what it is.

Tools do not create. Tools allow work to be done in a more effective manner. Used properly, it is an effective and very efficient vehicle to facilitate Knowledge Sharing, and Intranets do a wonderful job facilitating Knowledge Management. The following articles discuss the creation, evolution, and current uses of Intranets.

Adourian, A. and K. Schweyer. "Intranets and the Proactive Librarian." *Information Outlook* 01.07 (July 1997): 19-22.

Ba, S. L. et al. "Enterprise Decision Support Using Intranet Technology." *Decision Support Systems* 20.02 (June 1997): 99-134.

Ball, G. and P. Dilworth. "The Milton Keynes Clinical Intranet." *BJHC&IM: British Journal of Healthcare Computing & Information Management* 16.05: 42.

Campalans, A. et al. "Exploiting Intranets for Knowledge Management and Information Sharing." *Journal of Business and Financial Librarianship* 03.01 (1997): 27-39.

Cohen, Sacha. "Knowledge Management's Killer App." *Training & Development* 52.01 (January 1998): 50-57.

Dyer, J. H. and K. Nobeoka. "Creating and Managing a High-Performance Knowledge-Sharing Network: The Toyota Case." *Strategic Management Journal* 21.03 (March 2000): 345-367.

Fichter, Darlene. "Intranets: Librarians, Dive In!" *Online* 23.03 (May 1999): 107.

Fishenden, J. "Managing Intranets to Improve Business Process." *ASLIB Proceedings* 49.04 (April 1997): 90-96.

Fletcher, Liz. "Information Retrieval for Intranets: The Case for Knowledge Management." *Document World* 02.05 (September-October 1997): 32-34.

Ford, P. "Open Sesame!" *Business & Technology* (September 1999): 58.

Gardner, Dana. "Get Smart." *InfoWorld* 20.14 (06 April 1998): 97-98.

Gillman, P. "Evaluating the Intranet as Part of Your Knowledge Management Strategy." *ASLIB Proceedings* 49.02 (February 1997): 27-52.

Gladstone, Bryan and John Kawalek. "Problems on the Virtual Shop Floor." *Knowledge Directions* 01 (Spring 1999): 06-15.

Glickenhaus, Lee H. "Knowledge Transfer: Breaking Boundaries with Web-Based Networks." *Law Practice Management* 25.02 (01 March 1999): 24.

Goodfellow, Stephen F. "Document Management and Your Intranet: A Perfect Match." *OfficeSystems98* 16.04 (April 1999): 26-30.

Greengard, Samuel. "How to Fulfill Technology's Promise." *Workforce* 78.02 (February 1999): 10-19.

Haimila, Sandra. "PricewaterhouseCoopers Tracks Single Path to Content from a Myriad of Databases." *KMWorld* 09.05 (June 2000): 08.

Hoard, Bruce. "Intranet Success: The Dos." *KMWorld* 07.05 (27 April 2000): 32, 33.

"An Intranet Renaissance." *Training & Development* 53.08 (August 1999): 24.

"Intranets Are Not Instant Knowledge Management Systems." *Information Outlook* 02.09 (September 1998): 42.

"Intranets Fail as Knowledge Management Systems, Largely Because IT Doesn't Let Them Reach Far Enough, Analysts Warn." *Computerworld* 34.10 (2000): 28-31.

"Intranets: Transforming Information Management." *Information Outlook* 02.06 (June 1998): 13.

"IRC Notes." *Information Outlook* 02.09 (01 September 1998): 42.

Kepczyk, Roman H. "Intranets: The First Step to Knowledge Management." *Accounting Today* 13.21 (22 November 1999): 22, 25.

"Managing the Corporate Mind." *Internal Auditor* 55.02 (April 1998): 13-18.

Maurer, H. "Internet and Intranet Are More Than Just Support for Training and Education." *Elektrotechnik und Informationstechnik* 116.09 (1999): 491-494.

McCune, Jenny C. "MGMT Tech/Practices." *Management Review* 88.04 (01 April 1999): 10.

McQueen, Howard and Jean E. DeMatteo. "Intranets: New Opportunities for Information Professionals." *Online* 23.01 (January 1999): 14-22.

"Net Perceptions Delivers First Real-Time Personalization Product for Intranets and Knowledge Management." *PR Newswire* 0721 (October 06, 1999).

Pangaro, Paul. "Meta Data Can Turn an Enterprise Intranet Dream into a Corporate Reality." *InfoWorld* 21.30 (26 July 1999).

"Practical Solutions for Business Intranets." http://www.dynamicnet. net/news/white_papers/practicalintranets. htm

Robinson, Heather. "The Development of an Intranet as a Knowledge Management Tool." *Law Librarian* 31.02 (June 1999): 95-97.

Schrage, Michael. "When Best Practices Meet the Intranet, Innovation Takes a Holiday." *Fortune* 139.06 (29 March 1999): 198.

Scott, J. E. "Organizational Knowledge and the Intranet." *Decision Support Systems* 23.01 (May 1998): 03-17.

Smith, Laura B. "The Thinkers." *PC Week* 13.31 (05 August 1996): E01-E02.

Solomon, Marc. "What If You Gave an Online Party and Everyone Logged In? Or, How I Stopped Worrying and Learned To Love Intranets." *Searcher: The Magazine for Database Professionals* 05.04 (April 1997): 34-36, 38-40.

Stackpole, Beth. "The Pitch for Portals." *PC Week* 16.14 (05 April 1999): 73.

"A Talk with Patricia Foy: Director of Knowledge Strategies, Coopers & Lybrand." *Information Advisor* 02.01 (March 1998): 03-04.

Woodun, C. and R. O'Donnell. "Intranets: A Methodology for Implementation." McKenna, B. et al., eds. *Online Information 98: Proceedings*. Oxford: Learned Information Europe Ltd, 1998.

Woolliams, B. "Intranet Evolution: The Intranet in Your Business." McKenna, B. et al., eds. *Online Information 98. Proceedings* Oxford: Learned Information Europe Ltd, 1998.

KNOWLEDGE MANAGEMENT APPLICATION PACKAGES

Any field of endeavor, if it is alive and well, is constantly changing. As it changes, decisions must be made in order to keep the current hardware and software system as useful and up-to-date as possible. Every concept or every hardware or software system does not work for every Knowledge Management program. Decisions must be made as to what combination of human endeavor, process, and technology will best suit a given situation.

The Technology Boom, as mentioned earlier, has made a significant impact upon the field of Knowledge Management. Innovations such as DSL, groupware, Intranets, ISDN, LotusNotes, and shareware have allowed Knowledge Management professionals to customize the hardware and software they use. As everyone who uses computers knows, the most current applications are being modified and improved all of the time.

Every organization has some knowledge needs in common with other businesses. However, depending on its specific field of expertise, it will also have very specific needs, as well. The challenge in creating these Application Packages is to make them as flexible as possible. The systems need to be able to allow not only the creation of any specific functions a firm might need to have, but also be compatible with the hardware and software system the organization is currently using. The system must have the flexibility to expand as the needs of the Knowledge Management program grow, as well.

One error that many firms make is not taking advantage of the knowledge of those who use the system day in and day out. After all, who is better qualified to discuss a given job function and its corresponding system than those who use them day in and day out?

This group of articles not only discusses the technology that is available, it also provides some commentary on the suitability of these programs for various organizations, processes, and users.

Adams, Steve. "Knowledge Management." *Inform* 11.10 (November 1997): 10-13.

Adhikari, Richard. "On the GrapeVine." *InformationWeek* 647 (08 September 1997): 120-122.

Angus, Jeff et al. "Knowledge Management: Great Concept...But What Is It? Part 1 of 2." *InformationWeek* (16 March 1998): 58-60.

Angus, Jeff et al. "Knowledge Management: Great Concept...But What Is It? Part 2 of 2." *InformationWeek* (16 March 1998): 62-64.

Arunachalam, Subbiah. "Information and Knowledge in the Age of Electronic Communication: A Developing Country Perspective." *Journal of Information Science* 25.06 (1999): 465-476.

Blake, P. and C. Rabie. "Tooling Up for a Revolution." *Information World Review* 132 (January 1998): 15-16.

Bock, G. E. "Information Retrieval Tools for Knowledge Management." *Workgroup Computing Report* 21.01 (January 1998): 03-25.

Bock, G. E. "Knowledge Management Frameworks." *Workgroup Computing Report* 20.02 (February 1997): 03-22.

Cole-Gomolski, Barb. "Finding the Knowledge You Need." *Computerworld* 32.18 (04 May 1998): 69-70.

Dalrymple, Prudence. "Knowledge Management in the Health Sciences." Srikantaiah, Kanti and Michael E. D. Koenig, eds. *Knowledge Management for the Information Professional.* Medford, NJ: Information Today, 1999.

Darrow, Barbara, and Lee Copeland. "Lotus Looks to Break Ground in Knowledge Management." *Computer Reseller News* 773 (26 January 1998): 03-06.

Davenport, Tom. "The Knowledge Biz." *CIO* 11.04 (15 November 1997): 32-34.

Davenport, Tom. "We Have the Techknowledgy." *CIO* 09.21 (15 September 1996): 36-38.

DiCarlo, Lisa. "Lotus Hopes That Knowledge Is Power." *PC Week* (24 January 2000): 14.

Donoghue, Leigh P. et al. "Knowledge Management Strategies That Create Value." http://www.ac.com/overview/Outlook/1.99/currente4.html

Evans, Storm M. "Product Watch. New Products and Services Can Help You Improve Document Assembly, Time Reporting, Whiteboard Applications and 'Legal Knowledge' Management and Distribution." *Law Practice Management* 26.01 (01 January 2000): 24.

Fusaro, Roberta. "IBM/Lotus to Tackle Information Overload." *Computerworld* 32.26 (29 June 1998): 24.

Hibbard, Justin. "Ernst & Young Deploys App for Knowledge Management." *InformationWeek* (28 July 1997): 28.

Hibbard, Justin. "Lotus Takes on Knowledge Management." *InformationWeek* (02 February 1998): 26.

Hibbard, Justin. "Notes Goes Real-Time." *InformationWeek* (15 June 1998): 28.

Hodgson, Cynthia A. "Creating an Experts Database." *EContent* 22.05 (October-November 1999): 14-21.

"HP and Notable Solutions Inc. to Integrate Paper Documents INTO Microsoft Knowledge Management and Messaging Applications." *Business Wire* 0495 (01 February 2000).

Liebowitz, J. "Expert Systems: An Integral Part of Knowledge Management." *Kybernetes* 27.02 (1998): 170-175.

Marshak, D. S. "Organizational Knowledge Management: New Approaches from Information and PFN." *Workgroup Computing Report* 20.08 (August 1997): 03-19.

McNamara, Paul. "Lotus Gives Knowledge Management Brain Dump." *Network World* 15.26 (20 June 1998): 91.

McNamara, Paul. "Notes to Ride the Knowledge Management Wave." *Network World* 15.05 (02 February 1998): 10.

Melymuka, Kathleen. "Showing the Value of Brainpower." *Computerworld* 34.13 (27 March 2000): 58-59.

Ryske, Ellen J. and Theresa B. Sebastian. "From Library to Knowledge Center: The Evolution of a Technology Infocenter." Srikantaiah, Kanti and Michael E. D. Koenig, eds. *Knowledge Management for the Information Professional*. Medford, NJ: Information Today, 1999.

Schwartzwalder, Robert. "Manifesto: Seizing the Initiative in the Information Economy." *EContent* 23.01 (February-March 2000): 60-63.

Shadbolt, Nigel et al. "From Knowledge Engineering to Knowledge Management." *British Journal of Management* 10.04 (1999): 309-322.

Slack, Frances and Jennifer Rowley. "Pathways to Knowledge: A Perspective on Information Technology and Knowledge Delivery in Australia." *Journal of Librarianship and Information Science* 31.04 (December 1999): 197-203.

"Software for Knowledge Management." *Online* 21.05 (September-October 1997): 96.

Solomon, Marc. "Knowledge Management Tools for Knowledge Managers: Filling the Gap between Finding Information and Applying It." *Searcher: The Magazine for Database Professionals* 05.03 (March 1997): 10-14.

"Two Schools of Knowledge." *InformationWeek* (17 August 1998): 45.

Vedel, M. "Group Therapy—Groupware." *Application Development Advisor* 01.04 (March-April 1998): 52-55.

Walker, Christy. "Notes 5.0 Bets Is on Track: Lotus CEO Papows Focuses on Knowledge Management." *PC Week* 15.19 (11 May 1998): 19.

Walker, Christy. "New Ways to Make Data Pay: Knowledge Management Technology Improves Analysis and Decision-Making." *PC Week* 15.34 (24 August 1998): 14.

Ward, Jonathan. "In the Know." *Engineering* 240.09 (October 1999): 75-76.

Willett, Shawn and Lee Copeland. "Knowledge Management Key to IBM's Enterprise Plan." *Computer Reseller News* (27 July 1998): 01, 06.

KNOWLEDGE MANAGEMENT INITIATIVES

The newer the field, the faster and more numerous the changes within the field—especially if it is being adopted by more and more organizations. Throughout this Bibliography, virtually all of the discussion has linked Knowledge Management and the world of business. That is not to say that the only discipline that can apply Knowledge Management to its operations is business-related. In my opinion, the best thing about Knowledge Management is its ability to be applied to virtually any organization, whether it is non-profit or for profit, or in the private sector or in the public sector.

Even though two organizations are vastly different in their missions, goals, and objectives, it is certainly possible, if not probable that they have many knowledge requirements that are similar. The value of Knowledge Management is that its application is broad enough to allow interdisciplinary commonalities to be dealt with, and it can also be specific enough to deal with the proverbial one-in-a-million situation.

The existence and proliferation of interdisciplinary work has re-emphasized the fact that not all of the most current, usable information will come solely from within one given area of expertise. Therefore, Information Professionals must be aware of developments in other areas, being alert for improvements that begin in a different field, yet have uses that can be transferred to and assist in their work in a different field of study. The awareness of happenings in other areas of study is part of what makes Knowledge Management practitioners unique—the ability to see not only the developments within one function, but also take them, modify or improve their underlying mechanisms and apply these functions to other, seemingly unrelated operations.

This group of writings is an effort to provide an overview of some of the more recent programs and innovations in Knowledge Management being pursued in various applications.

Anthes, Gary H. "Learning How to Share." *Computerworld* 32 (23 February 1998): 75-77.

Ash, Jerry. "State of KM Practice among Early Adopters." *Knowledge Inc.* (August 1997).

Barron, Daniel D. "Knowledge Management for the New Millennium: The Next Step for School Library Media Specialists." *School Library Media Activities Monthly* 16.05 (January 2000): 48-51.

Bernhardt, S. A. and G. A. McCulley. "Knowledge Management and Pharmaceutical Development Teams: Using Writing to Guide Science." *IEEE Transactions on Professional Communication* 43.01 (March 2000): 22-34.

Boone, Mary E. "A Group Brain is Better than One." *Sales & Marketing Management* 151.11 (November 1999): 141-142.

Boulet, Michelle and Brian Hamilton. "The Issue Is: Knowledge Management — A Discussion Paper." http://jobs.gc.ca/prcb/rd/knowledge/km_issue_e.htm

Buckman, Robert H., Ph. D. "Knowledge Sharing at Buckman Labs." *Journal of Business Strategy* 19.01 (January 1998): 10-15.

Bukowitz, Wendi R. and Ruth L. Williams. "Looking through the Knowledge Glass." *CIO* 13.02 (15 October 1999): 76-85.

Burn, Janice M. and Colin Ash. "Knowledge Management Strategies for Virtual Organisations." *Information Resources Management Journal* 13.01 (January-March 2000): 15-23.

Carrillo, J. E. and C. Gaimon. "Improving Manufacturing Performance through Process Change and Knowledge Creation." *Management Science* 46.02 (February 2000): 265-288.

Cerny, Keith. "Making Local Knowledge Global." *Harvard Business Review* (May-June 1996): 22.

Cole-Gomolski, Barb. "Corporate Strategist: Gordon Petrash." *Computerworld* 32.01 (29 December 1997-05 January 1998): 49-50.

Collins, Rod. "Auditing in the Knowledge Era." *Internal Auditor* 56.03 (June 1999): 26-31.

Davenport, Thomas H. et al. "Successful Knowledge Management Projects." *Sloan Management Review* 39.02 (Winter 1998): 43-57.

David, Ian. "Doing the Knowledge." *Professional Engineering* 11.11 (10 June 1998): 29-30.

Davis, Michael C. "Knowledge Management." *Information Strategy: The Executive's Journal* 15.01 (Fall 1998): 11-22.

Dearstyne, Bruce W. "Records Management of the Future: Anticipate, Adapt, and Succeed." *Information Management Journal* 33.04 (October 1999): 04-18.

Dillon, Martin. "Knowledge Management Opportunities for Libraries and Universities." *Library and Information Science Annual* 07 (1999): 03-11.

Dorfman, Peter. "Towards a Knowledge-Based Customer Support Program." *Knowledge Management Review* 01.04 (1998): 24-33.

Elliott, Susan. "APQC Conference Attendees Discover the Value and Enablers of a Successful KM Program." *Knowledge Management in Practice* (December 1996-January 1997): 01-05.

Emmott, Lyle C. "Knowledge Management Systems: Maintenance on the Front Lines." *Plant Engineering* 53.09 (September 1999): 40-44.

Emmott, Lyle C. "Management Side of Engineering." *Plant Engineering* 53.09 (September 1999): 40.

Eppler, Martin J. and Oliver Sukowski. "Managing Team Knowledge: Core Processes, Tools and Enabling Factors." *European Management Journal* 18.03 (2000): 334.

"Finance and Economics: Knowledge Gap." *Economist* (16 October 1999): 80-81.

Flanagan, Robert J. "Knowledge Management in Global Organizations in the 21st Century." *HRMagazine* 44.11 (1999): 54-55.

Githens, Gregory D. "Capturing Project Requirements and Knowledge." *PM Network* 14.02 (February 2000): 49-50, 53, 55-59.

Gosling, Paul. "Patterns of Evidence." *Knowledge Management* (December 1999-January 2000): 10-11.

Gottschalk, F. "Use of IT for Knowledge Management in Law Firms." http://elj.warwick.ac.uk/jilt

"Government-Best Practice-Audit Office Guides to Better Management-Years of Knowledge Condensed into Practical Guides." *Australian CPA* 70.05 (2000): 78-79.

Graves, William and Bud Sonka. "Plenary Sessions—Moving the Network Revolution in Knowledge Management beyond Random Acts of Progress." *The Serials Librarian* 38.01 (2000): 25-30.

Hafstad, .Sissel. "The Knowledge Management Process in a Business School Environment." *Business Information Review* 14.03 (September 1997): 135-140.

Haimila, Sandra. "Harvesting Pure Knowledge for the National Organic Program." *KMWorld* 08.02 (February 1999): 28.

Hamilton, F. "Knowledge Management in the Oil and Gas Industry." *Information Management Report* (April 1997): 18-19.

Hibbard, Justin and Karen M. Carrillo. "Knowledge Revolution: Getting Employees to Share What They Know Is No Longer a Technology Challenge. It's a Corporate Culture Challenge." *InformationWeek* (05 January 1998): 49-54.

Hildebrand, Carol. "Experts for Hire." *CIO* (15 April 1995): 32-40.

"Management with E & Y Kenneth Leventhal Real Estate Group." *Real Estate Forum* 53.03 (March 1998): 92-93.

Jahnke, Art. "Share Ware." *CIO* 11.18 (01 July 1998): 10.

Johnson, Donald E. L. "Making Knowledge Management a Priority." *Health Care Strategic Management* 15.04 (April 1997): 02-03.

Knapp, Ellen M. "Knowledge Management." *Business and Economic Review* 44.04 (July-September 1998): 03-06.

"Knowledge Management: How to Make It Work." *Management Today* (August 1997): 31.

"Knowledge Management: The Era of Shared Ideas." *Forbes* 160.06 (22 September 1997): F28.

Koch, Christopher. "Reap What You Know." *CIO* 10.14 (01 May 1997): 118-122.

"Leveraging Knowledge at the Public Service Commission of Canada: A Discussion Paper Prepared for Research Directorate Public Service Commission of Canada." http://jobs.gc.ca/prcb/rd/knowledge/km_psc_e.htm

Lohrke, C. T. et al. "Analytical Laboratory: World Class Distinction with World-Wide Connection: From Managing Instrumentation to Managing Knowledge." *Laboratory Automation and Information Management* 34.01 (October 1999): 41-49.

Manville, Brook and Nathaniel Foote. "Harvest Your Workers' Knowledge." *Datamation* 42.13 (July 1996): 78-82.

Mariotti, John. "Four Formulas for Success." *Industry Week* 248.18 (04 October 1999): 66.

Martin, Justin. "Are You as Good as You Think You Are?" *Fortune* 134.06 (30 September 1996): 142-152.

Martin, W. J. "Approaches to the Measurement of the Impact of Knowledge Management Programmes." *Journal of Information Science* 26.01 (2000): 21-27.

Martinez, Michelle Neely. "The Collective Power of Employee Knowledge." *HR Magazine* 43 (February 1998): 88-94.

May, Thornton. "Sailing the Seven C's of Knowledge Management." *Insights Perspectives* (01 April 1996).

McKenna, Brian. "Reaching New Audiences, Speaking New Languages." *Knowledge Management* (December 1999-January 2000): 21-23.

Mineau, G. W. et al. "Conceptual Modeling for Data and Knowledge Management." *Data & Knowledge Engineering* 33.02 (2000): 137-168.

Mullin, Rick. "Knowledge Management: A Cultural Evolution." *Journal of Business Strategy* 17.05 (September-October 1996): 56-59.

Nickerson-Tietze, Donna J. "Community-Based Management for Sustainable Fisheries Resources in Phang-nga Bay, Thailand." *Coastal Management* 28.01 (2000): 65.

Odem, Peggy and Carla O'Dell. "Invented Here: How Sequent Computer Publishes Knowledge." *Journal of Business Strategy* 19 (January-February 1998).

O'Leary, D. E. "Using AI in Knowledge Management: Knowledge Bases and Ontologies." *IEEE Intelligent Systems* 13.03 (May-June 1998): 34-39.

Olonoff, Neil. "Knowledge Management and Project Management." *PM Network* 14.02 (February 2000): 61-64.

Payne, Laurie W. "Managing Knowledge at Monsanto Brings Excitement to the Word 'Change'." *Knowledge Management in Practice* (October-November 1997): 01-08.

Payne, Laurie W. "Making Knowledge Management Real at the National Security Agency." *Knowledge Management in Practice* (August-September 1997): 01-08.

Phillips, Tessy and Mike Vollmer. "Knowledge Management in the Current Marketplace." *Oil and Gas Journal* 98.13 (27 March 2000): 04.

Platt, Nina. "Knowledge Management: Can It Exist in a Law Office?" Srikantaiah, Kanti and Michael E. D. Koenig, eds. *Knowledge Management for the Information Professional*. Medford, NJ: Information Today, 1999.

Prokesch, Steven E. "Unleashing the Power of Learning: An Interview with British Petroleum's John Browne." *Harvard Business Review* (September-October 1997): 146-148.

Quinn, James Brian. "Strategic Outsourcing: Leveraging Knowledge Capabilities." *Sloan Management Review* 40.04 (Summer 1999): 09-21.

Ratzek, W. and M. Zwicker. "Integrated Knowledge Management as the Future Strategic Success Factor?" *NFD Information—Wissenschaft und Praxis* 50.06 (September 1999): 339-346.

Sacks, Jennifer. "Managing Knowledge: How the Delphi Group Seeks to Help Business." *LatinFinance* 110 (September 1999): 49.

Schein, Esther. "Keeping the Motor Humming with Data." *PC Week* 15.06 (09 February 1998): 75-77.

Sprague, Robert D. "Creating Knowledge Management Systems for Law Firms." *Los Angeles Lawyer* 21.11 (01 February 1999): 15.

Strawser, Corydon. "Building Effective Knowledge Management Solutions." *Journal of Healthcare Information Management* 14.01 (2000): 73-80.

Stucki, Heinz and Gregg L. Andrews. "Knowledge-Based Economic Development: A Simplified Model for Practitioners." *Economic Development Review* 16.02 (1999): 97-100.

Taylor, Andrew and Tom Oates. "Technology as Knowledge: Towards a New Perspective on Knowledge Management in Electronics." *International Journal of Technological Management* 11.03-04 (1996): 296-314.

Tidline, Toniya J. "The Mythology of Information Overload." *Library Trends* 47.03 (Winter 1999): 485-506.

"Unearthing Your Company's Hidden Knowledge: How to Create a Best Practice Identification System." *Business Wire* 0508 (05 January 2000).

Vale, Mark. "Leveraging Knowledge at the Public Service Commission of Canada: A Discussion Paper." http://www.psc-cfp.gc.ca/library/know ledge/webdoc1.htm

Velker, Lee. "Knowledge: The Chevron Way." *KMWorld* 08.02 February 1999): 20-21.

Voorhees, Mark. "If Only We Knew Then What We Know Now." *National Law Journal* 22.17 (20 December 1999): B17.

Wah, Louisa. "Making Knowledge Stick." *Management Review* 88.05 (May 1999): 24-29.

Weigend, A. S. et al. "Exploiting Hierarchy in Text Categorization." *Information Retrieval* 01.03 (1999): 193-216.

Whitehead, Mark. "Collection Time." *People Management* 05.21 (28 October 1999): 68-69.

Woytek, Reinhard. "Indigenous Knowledge for Development." Knowledge and Learning Center, Africa Region, World Bank. (November 1998): 01-05.

Yeh, Jian-Hua et al. "Content and Knowledge Management in a Digital Library and Museum." *Journal of the American Society for Information Science* 51.04 (01 March 2000): 371-379.

Ziarko, Wojciech. "Discovery through Rough Set Theory." *Communications of the ACM* 42.11 (November 1999): 54.

KNOWLEDGE MANAGEMENT AND TRAINING

New equipment, new or changed job functions, new employees, new pro-cedures, and new subjects of study—all of these things require training to pro-vide both current users and new employees with the necessary skills to be able to use the change agents in the most effective and efficient ways possible.

Knowledge Management is the perfect vehicle to increase the value of employee training. By its very nature, Knowledge Management seeks to cre-ate an environment that includes Shared Knowledge, functions that can be shared throughout the organization. What better place to start involving employees in a Knowledge Management program than in Initial or Continuation Training? If a new employee is given training emphasizing the value and necessity of Knowledge Management, then he or she will work using Knowledge Management as a foundation.

The main issue with change that most current employees in an organiza-tion have is the alleged value of all of the changes. By using Knowledge Management techniques in Continuation Training; e. g., the creation of a Best Practices database, or by demonstrating the benefits of Shared Knowledge, the skeptical employee can see first-hand the true value of Knowledge Management, which is to make him or her a more effective and skilled employee. An employee who has performed a given function for an extended period of time often forgets to pass on relevant Tacit Knowledge to new employees. Is it an intentional slight? No. After a period of time, many opera-tions become so ingrained that they become automatic—almost instinctive, and so the training employee doesn't think to pass this information to others. As a result, the previously skeptical employee can become an agent for change rather than someone who goes back to the workplace decrying the change as yet another soon-to-fail management technique.

The flexibility and innovations that have made Knowledge Management such a valuable tool in the business world can make a substantial contribu-tion in the area of Human Relations and Training as well. After all, how much value does an untrained or under-trained employee have?

"@work-Best of the Web—We Pick 20 Top Training—and Workplace-Related Websites about e-learning, Knowledge Management, Small Business, and More." *Training & Development* 54.05 (2000): 26-33.

Adler, Paul S. and Robert E. Cole. "Designed for Learning: A Tale of Two Auto Plants." *Sloan Management Review* 34.03 (Spring 1993): 85-94.

Alonzo, Vincent. "Ernst & Young LLP." *Incentive* 172.06 (June 1998): 26-27.

Bassi, Laurie J. et al. "Training Industry Trends 1997." *Training & Development* 51 (November 1997): 46-50.

Bennett, James C. "Achieving Professional Excellence for a New Century." *Information Management Journal* 33.02 (April 1999): 36-42.

Calvacca, Lorraine. "Training for the Bottom Line." *Folio* 27.04 (15 March 1998): 32-34.

Chaudron, David. "Global Training Gets High-Tech at Buckman Labs." *HR Focus* 75.04 (April 1998): S12.

Densford, Lynn E. "General Motors University: Overseeing Training for 650,000." *Corporate University Review* 06.02 (March 1998): 08-09.

Eisenberg, Howard. "Reengineering and Dumbsizing: Mismanagement of the Knowledge Resource." *Quality Progress* 30.05 (May 1997): 57-64.

Galagan, Patricia. "Bullet Train." *Training & Development* 53.07 (July 1999): 22-28.

Houlder, Vanessa. "How to Turn an Average Worker into a Star." *Financial Times* (23 May 1997): 17-18.

Kenyon, Henry S. "Volvo University: Building a Culture of Customer Satisfaction." *Corporate University Review* (01 February 1998).

Kleiner, A. and G. Ruth. "How to Make Experience Your Company's Best Teacher." *Harvard Business Review* 75.05: 172-177.

Koenig, M. E. D. and Kanti Srikantaiah. "Education for Knowledge Management." *Information Services & Use* 19.01: 17-31.

Levin, Rich. "Train at the Speed of Change." *InformationWeek* (08 June 1998): 01A-05A.

Masie, Elliot. "Embedded Learning and Support Is Worthy Investment." *Computer Reseller News* (03 January 2000): 35.

"Measuring Training's Contribution to Intellectual Capital." *Training* 35 (March 1998): 14-16.

Nofsinger, Mary Ann. "Training and Re-Training Reference Professionals: Core Competencies for the 21st Century." *The Reference Librarian* 64:09.

Petrovic, Otto et al. "Learning Aspects of Knowledge Management and New Technologies." *Journal of European Industrial Training* 22.07 (1998): 277-288.

Rossett, Allison. "Knowledge Management Meets Analysis." *Training & Development* 53.05 (May 1999): 62-68.

Smythe, David. "Facing the Future: Preparing New Information Professionals." *Information Management Journal* 33.02 (April 1999): 44-46.

Srikantaiah, Kanti. *LIS 880 Knowledge Management Course Syllabus: Fall 1998.* Dominican University, Graduate School of Library and Information Science, River Forest, IL.

Stamps, David. "Enterprise Training: This Changes Everything: Just When You Thought Reengineering Had Run Its Course, It's Back Again. This Time It Comes with a Knowledge Management Twist That Heralds Real

Changes for How Organizational Learning May Happen in the Future." *Training* 36.01 (1999): 40.

Steen, Margaret. "Training for the Future." *InfoWorld* 100.01 (26 October 1998).

Switzer, John. "Managing Human Capital." *Banking Strategies* 72 (November-December 1996): 50-55.

Van Braekel, Pieter. "Teaching Information Management via a Web-Based Course." *The Electronic Library* 17.06 (December 1999): 389-394.

KNOWLEDGE MANAGEMENT ECOMMERCE AND .COMS

Five years ago, approximately 20 percent of Fortune 500 companies had Web sites. Now, that number is 100 percent. Why? Because the value of a presence on the World Wide Web has been proven to be a prerequisite to doing business in the 21st Century.

Amazon.com, ebay.com, E*TRADE.com—the new blood in the business world has a presence on the Web. And now, even old, established firms like Marshall Field's (www.marshallfields.com) have joined in this trend. Is it going to end? Not likely. In fact, it is projected that eCommerce will increase exponentially in the future. New companies, old companies, companies trying to renew or re-invent themselves are realizing that there is a vast, virtually untapped market in cyberspace.

The question now becomes how to be successful in this new medium. Obviously, old procedures and policies will not work in this new, rapidly changing environment. How does an organization provide quality service in a virtual environment without alluring merchandise displays or helpful sales staff? The ambiance, the individualized customer service, and the physical presence of a store will no longer exist. Does that mean that customers will accept poor service since the transaction is completed on the computer? Absolutely not.

Knowledge Management is the key to keeping customer loyalty while changing customer's perceptions about this new environment. Employees and managers will have to learn a new set of skills to satisfy the new needs that this medium creates. The effective and efficient use of knowledge is more important than ever. Should a problem occur with a shipment, there may not be a "manager" to whom the customer can complain in person. The lack of interpersonal contact exists, but by using Knowledge Management techniques ranging from Best Practices to Shared Knowledge, the problems can be rectified without any long-term damage to the customer-provider relationship.

These articles look at the fleeting present and the long-term future of the phenomenon that allows consumers to go "into" almost any store or business without leaving their home or office.

"AMS Study Finds Vast Opportunity for Telecommunications Firms to Exploit eCommerce." *PR Newswire* 6105 (25 August 1999).

"AMS Taps Renowned Experts to Launch Electronic-Commerce-in-Government Initiatives." *PR Newswire* 3568 (02 August 1999).

Berry, John. "Traditional Training Fades in Favor of E-Learning: Internet Economy Demands a More Flexible Training Approach." *InternetWeek* (14 February 2000): 33.

Bloor, Robin. "Dealing with eCommerce." *Computing* (20 May 1999): 28.

Brien, John P. "Working the New Digital Information Economy: Mastering Customer Relationships; Some Management Strategies for Online Development." *LASIE* 30.02 (June 1999): 27-33.

Buchanan, Doug. "Finance One Makes Moves to Raise Internet Commerce." *Business First-Columbus* 15.22 (22 January 1999): 05.

Cahners Publishing Company. "Internet-Ation without Taxation." *Electronic News* 44 (August 10, 1998): 54.

Carr, Nicholas G. "Redesigning Business." *Harvard Business Review* 77.06 (November-December 1999): 19.

Chabrow, Eric. "Seeking the Deeper Path to E-Success—Companies That Use a Combination of E-Business Best Practices and Value Commitment as Much as Investment Are Realizing Returns in Terms of More Customers, Lower Costs, and Market Creation." *InformationWeek* (06 March 2000): 48.

Charlesworth, Andrew. "How to…Build an eCommerce System." *Computing* (04 December 1997): 66.

Choy, Jorina. "'Strong Foundation and Cultural Values' Key to E-Success." *Asia Computer Weekly* (30 November 1999).

Chuck, Lysabeth B. "The Virtual Taxman Cometh: Looming Issues for Internet Commerce." *Searcher: The Magazine for Database Professionals* 06 (May 1998): 36-44.

"Companies Prepare for eCommerce." *Marketing* (16 July 1998): 18.

Currie, Antony. "We Gotta Get out of This Place…" *Euromoney* 371 (March 2000): 06.

Dalton, Gregory and Sean Gallagher. "Online Data's Fine Line." *InformationWeek* (29 March 1999): 18-20.

De Feo, Joseph. "Fashion Will Suffocate IT." *Computing* (15 October 1998): 34.

Drury, James and Don Van Doren. "Realistic Choices for Web-Based Call Centers." *Business Communications Review* 29.06 (June 1999): 56-61.

Dudman, Jane. "Putting Value into the Chain." *Computing* (26 November 1998): 53.

"e.biz." *Business Week* (05 June 2000): EB01-EB126.

"e-commerce." *Fortune Technology Guide* (Summer 2000): 40-187.

"E-commerce News." *Accounting Technology* 15.07 (August 1999): 16.

"eCommerce.com and Extant-Asia to Launch eCommerce Portal for China." *Business Wire* 0082 (03 January 2000).

Evans, Philip and Thomas S. Wurster. "Getting Real About Virtual Commerce." *Harvard Business Review* 77.06 (November-December 1999): 85.

Everett, Cath. "Ecommerce Set to Snowball." *Computing* (16 July 1998): 18.

Farrell, Nick. "Internet to Become 'Dominant Medium'." *Computing* (01 October 1998): 32.

"The Future of Internet Commerce on Display at iEC." *Business Wire* 1193 (24 February 2000).

Gingrande, Arthur. "Web Marketing Boosts DIM Sales." *KMWorld* 07.08 (08 June 1998): 22-23, 27.

Hardy, Michael and Frances Horner. "Billabongs, Dugongs, Internet, and Tax." *OECD Observer* (January 1999): 15.

"How to Succeed in the New Knowledge Economy: Linking Knowledge Management to Corporate Strategy." *Business Wire* 1541 (31 January 2000).

Huber, Nick. "Cashing in on Cyber Money." *Computing* (19 February 1998): 24.

Jones, Chris. "E-commerce Extends Its Reach: Established Vendors Use Respected Brands to Attract Users." *InfoWorld* 18.42 (14 October 1996): 06.

Kessler, Mark. "India Logs on, E-Biz Responds." http://www.wired.com/news/technology/0,1282,33041,00.html

Kirby, Peter S. "Plug and Play: The Future of eCommerce." *Electronic News* (07 December 1998): 08.

Krapf, Eric. "Can Businesses Find Common Ground for eCommerce?" *Business Communications Review* 29.04 (April 1999): 43-46.

Kruger, Peter. "Driving Home an Opportunity." *Communications International* 26.03 (March 1999): 39-40.

Lambeth, Jonathan. "Europe Faces eCommerce Revolution." *Computing* (17 September 1998): 22-23.

Leadbeater, Charles. "It's Not Just the Economy, Stupid." *New Statesman* (27 September 1999): iv.

Lewis, Ted. "Jump-Starting the Global Vending Machine." *Computer* (June 1999): 120-121.

Madden, John. "Ernst & Young Weaves e-Com into Consulting." *PC Week* 16.11 (15 March 1999): 52.

Malhotra, Yogesh. "Knowledge Management for E-Business Performance: Advancing Information Strategy to 'Internet Time'." *Information Strategy: The Executive's Journal* 16.04 (Summer 2000): 05-16.

Malim, George. "Ecommerce a Priority." *Telecommunications* 33.08 (August 1999): 11,16.

Marzulli, Tony. "Achieving a Healthy e-Business Solution: Key Attributes to Cutting-Edge E-business Management Systems Are Connectivity, Knowledge and Performance." *Health Management Technology* 21.01 (01 January 2000): 18.

McGrath, Peter. "Knowing You All Too Well." *Newsweek* 133.13 (29 March 1999): 48.

McMillin, Kevin. "Knowledge Management Lessons Aiding E-Commerce Growth." *Oil and Gas Journal* 98.13 (27 March 2000): 02.

McWilliams, Gary and Marcia Stepanek. "Knowledge Management: Taming the Info Monster." *Business Week* (22 June 1998): 170-172.

Messner, Kelly. "Turning eChaos into eCommerce." *Upside Online Trading Networks Supplement* (January 1999): 08.

Nelson, Matthew. "Security, Internet Commerce on the Menu at ICE." *InfoWorld* 20.13 (30 March 1998): 19.

Newman, Nathan. "The Great Internet Tax Drain." *Technology Review* 99 (May-June 1996): 24-30.

Ojala, Marydee. "Information Professionals Meet Ecommerce." *Online* 23.05 (September-October 1999): 82.

Pigott, Sylvia E. A. "Internet Commerce and Knowledge Management: The Next Megatrends." *Business Information Review* 14.04 (December 1997): 169-172.

Poynder, Richard. "Out of the Labs and into Profit." *Knowledge Management* (December 1999-January 2000): 26-30.

"Profiting with the New Knowledge Economy: Recognition and Sharing of Best Practices." *Business Wire* 1216 (07 January 2000).

Randall, Robert F. "Internet Will Speed Europe Market Harmonization." *Strategic Finance* 80.11 (May 1999): 20.

Ranger, Steve. "High Price to Pay for eCommerce." *Computing* (23 July 1998): 18.

Robinson, Dan. "Ecommerce in the Grip of a Taxing Problem." *Computing* (11 June 1998): 28.

Rosa, Jerry. "Integration Behemoths Move at E-Speed." *Computer Reseller News* (10 January 2000): 01.

Sabbagh, Dan. "Fate of eCommerce Lies in Labour Hands." *Computing* (21 January 1999): 27.

Sabbagh, Dan. "More Questions Than Answers." *Computing* (08 April 1999): 22.

Soete, Luc and Bas ter Weel. "Cybertax." *Futures* 30.09 (November 1998): 853.

Solomon, Marc. "Next Generation E-Business Intelligence: E for External." *Searcher: The Magazine for Database Professionals* 07.10 (November 1999): 26-32.

Turek, Norbert. "E-Commerce Counts on Servers: Choosing the Right Commerce-Server Vendor Is a Critical Decision." *InformationWeek* (13 September 1999).

Turner, Mary Johnston. "Bandwidth and Browsers Power Enhanced Services." *Business Communications Review* 29.05 (May 1999): 49-52.

Vlosky, Richard P. "eBusiness in the Forest Products Industry." *Forest Products Journal* 49.10 (October 1999): 12-21.

Walker, Richard W. "The Road to e-Commerce is a Long One." *Government Computer News* 18.13 (03 May 1999): 52.

Yates, M. "eEurope—eCommerce Revolution or Damp Squib?" *Colloquim Digest* 460 (1998).

"ZDNet and Creative Good Launch 'E-Business Best Practices', Providing Real-Life Examples of eCommerce Do's and Don'ts." *PR Newswire* 4312 (19 July 1999).

Zoellick, Bill. "The Knowledge Marketplace." *KMWorld* 07.12 (November 1998): 13.

KNOWLEDGE MANAGEMENT CHAPTERS IN CONFERENCE PROCEEDINGS

The cycle of creation starts in the laboratory with a concept, a thought. It then moves to discussion of the concept, process, or theory with one's peers. This occasionally causes the researcher to re-evaluate some of his or her concepts or perhaps the approaches used. The next stage is usually the presentation of new ideas or utilities at conferences. The additions, changes, or refutations that occur in the arena of debate are among the most important stages of the process. Next is the publication of journal articles that can foster further debate and improvement. At this point, the subject matter is in the "real world." Virtually all scholarship projects have used this cycle to help further the knowledge of their respective disciplines.

Presentation of papers at conferences and seminars allows a concentrated group of professionals to hear what possibilities the new changes and innovations in a given field have to offer. The primary value of these meetings is to put the collective intellects of these individuals together so that the communication is instantaneous and personal. Electronic communication is considered by many to be the be-all and end-all in terms of exchanging ideas and information. Yes, it is fast, and yes, it is inexpensive, but it does not allow for the most important part of communication—face-to-face conversation. Gestures, facial expressions, and posture cannot be conveyed in print. The majority of meaning in communication takes place non-verbally. This is the major benefit of conferences and seminars. Another benefit of face-to-face communication is instantaneous feedback and response. Oftentimes, a question occurs to someone reading correspondence. The reader is interrupted, has to handle an unrelated situation, comes back and realizes that he or she has forgotten the question. Speaking to the writer in person provides a greater opportunity for specific conversation and immediate response.

These Conference Papers will be an excellent guide to cutting-edge information that has been presented at various conferences of various groups who are interested in and pursuing Knowledge Management.

Aha, David W. et al., Co-Chairs. *Exploring Synergies of Knowledge Management & Case-Based Reasoning* Menlo Park, CA: AAAI Press, 1999.

Albert, Judith. "Nuts and Bolts of Knowledge Management for Information Professionals." *Proceedings of the National Online Meeting* 19.01 (12 May 1998): 06-15.

Barker, K. and M. T. Ozsu, eds. *Proceedings of 5th International Conference on Information and Knowledge Management.* New York: ACM, 1996.

Becerra-Fernandez, I. et al. "Knowledge Management: Redefining Corporate Assets." *Proceedings of the Seventh International Conference on Management of Technology* (1998).

Benjamins, V. R. et al. "Knowledge Management through Ontologies." Reimer, Ulrich, ed. *PAKM '98, Practical Aspects of Knowledge Management: Proceedings of the Second International Conference, Basel, Switzerland, October 29-30, 1998.* [Zurich]: [s.n.], 1998: 05.1-05.12.

Bharat, Krishna and Andrei Broder. "A Technique for Measuring the Relative Size and Overlap of Public Web Search Engines. *Proceedings of the 7th International World Wide Web Conference.* Brisbane: Elsevier Science, 1998. http://decweb.ethz.ch

Boersma, J. S. K. T. and R. A. Stegwee. *"Exploring the Issues in Knowledge Management." Proceedings of the 1996 Information Resources Management Association International Conference.* Hershey, PA: Idea Group Publishing, 1996.

Boynton, A. "How to Get Started with Knowledge Management." *Exploring Opportunities in Knowledge Management, Knowledge Management Symposium: Leveraging Knowledge for Business Impact.* Sydney: IBM Consulting Group, 1996.

Brown, Stephanie et al. "Ground Truth, Learning Networks in the Army." *Proceedings of the Academy of Management Annual Meeting, 1997.*

Choo, C. W. "National Computer Policy Management in Singapore: Planning an Intelligent Island." *Forging New Partnerships in Information: Proceedings of the 58th Annual Meeting of the American Society for Information Science.* Medford, NJ: Information Today, 1995.

David, Paul A. "Knowledge, Property, and the System Dynamics of Technological Change." Summers, Lawrence M. and Shekhar Shah, eds. *Proceedings of the World Bank Annual Conference on Development Economics.* Washington, DC: World Bank, 1993.

Dysart, Jane I. "The SCIP Conference for CI Professionals: Conference Coverage Focused on Knowledge-Based Strategies for Success." *Information Today* 15.05 (May 1998): 23-25.

Field, J. "Information + Technology + You Equals Knowledge Management." *Proceedings of the 13th Annual Computers in Libraries '98 in Cooperation with the Special Libraries Association.* Medford, NJ: Information Today, 1998: 60-62.

Field, M. "How to Dine Free at the Hilton." *Library Association Record* 100.03 (March 1998): 124.

Friedman, Sam. "Knowledge Sharing Gives Agents an Edge." *National Underwriter* 103.19 (10 May 1999): 09.

Gaines, Brian et al., eds. *Artificial Intelligence in Knowledge Management: Papers from the Spring 1997 Symposium.* Menlo Park, CA: AAAI Press, 1997.

Germany European Knowledge Acquisition Workshop. *Knowledge Acquisition and Management. 11th European Workshop, EKAW '99 Dagsuhl Castle, Germany, May, 1999: Proceedings.* Berlin: Springer-Verlag, 1999.

Hanley, S. "Building Knowledge-Based Communities of Practice: Lessons Learned from a Knowledge Management Success." *Online Information 98: Proceedings.* Oxford: Learned Information Europe Ltd, 1998.

Hardin, Steve. "Human Work in a Computer Age." *Bulletin of the American Society for Information Science* 25.02 (December 1998-January 1999): 13-15.

Harvey, Michael et al. "Implementing Intra-Organizational Learning: A Phased-Model Approach Supported by Intranet Technology." *European Management Journal* 16.03 (June 1998): 341-354.

Hildreth, P. et al. "Knowledge Management: Are We Missing Something?" Brooks, L. and C. Kimble, eds. *Proceedings of the 4th UKAIS Conference.* Maidenhead, UK: McGraw-Hill Publising Co., 1999.

Kappes, Sandra and Beverly Thomas. *A Model for Knowledge Worker Information Support.* Champaign, IL: Construction Engineering Research Laboratories, 1993.

Kappes, Sandra et al. *Document Management for the Knowledge Worker System.* Champaign, IL: Construction Engineering Research Laboratories, 1995.

Khosrowpour, M., ed. *Proceedings of 1998 Information Resources Management Association International Conference.* Hershey, PA: Idea Group Publishing, 1998.

Klahr, P. "Knowledge Management on a Global Scale." *Proceedings of the 1997 Spring Symposium on Artificial Intelligence in Knowledge Management.* Stanford, CA: AAAI Press, 1997: 82-85.

Klempa, M. J. and J. A. Britt. "Managing Information Technology: An Acquisition/Diffusion Contingency Model Integrating Organization Culture, Organization Learning, and Knowledge Sharing." *Emerging Information Technologies for Competitive Advantage and Economic Development: Proceedings of 1992 Information Resources Management Association International Conference.* Hershey, PA: Idea Group Publishing, 1992.

Koenig, Michael. "The 1998 Conference Board Conference." *Information Today* 15.07 (July-August 1998): 13, 51.

Koenig, Michael E. D. "Libraries and Their Impact Upon Productivity." *IFLA Pre-Conference Workshop* (14 August 1995): 01-32.

Komorowski, Jan, ed. and Jan Zytkow. *Principles of Data Mining and Knowledge Discovery. First European Symposium, Pkdd '97 Trondheim, Norway, 24-27 June 1997: Proceedings.* Berlin: Springer-Verlag, 1997.

Koren, Johan. "Knowledge Mobilisation in Rural Regions: The Public Library as Knowledge Catalyst." Paper submitted to the Third National Conference on Library Research, Fornebu, Oslo, Norway. (18-19 January 1999).

Kotnour, T. et al. "Determining the Benefit of Knowledge Management Activities." IEEE Systems, Man & Cybernetics Society Staff, *1997 IEEE International Conference on Systems, Man, & Cybernetics, Vol. 1.* New York: IEEE, 1997.

Leake, D. et al. "Acquiring Case Adaptation Knowledge: A Hybrid Approach." *Proceedings of the Thirteenth National Conference on Artificial Intelligence.* Menlo Park, CA: AAAI Press, 1996: 684-689.

LeFaure, Skip. "The 1998 Conference of Knowledge Management and Organizational Learning." Presentation at the Conference Board Conference, Chicago. (15 April 1998).

Luger, G. F., ed. *Proceedings. Artificial Intelligence and Manufacturing Workshop. State of the Art and State of the Practice.* Menlo Park, CA: AAAI Press, 1998.

Malhotra, Yogesh. "Knowledge Management in Inquiring Organizations." *Proceedings of the 3rd Americas Conference on Information Systems.* (15-17 August 1997).

Malwad, N. M. et al., eds. *Towards the New Information Society of Tomorrow: Innovations, Challenges and Impact: Papers Presented at the 49th FID Conference and Congress.* New Delhi: Indian National Science Documentation Centre, 1998.

Matarazzo, J. M. "Measuring the Value of the Corporate Information Resource." Raitt, David Z. et al., eds. *Online Information 97 Proceedings. 21st International Online Information Meeting.* Oxford: Learned Information Europe Ltd, 1997.

Maurer, F. and B. Dellen. "A Concept for an Internet-Based Process-Oriented Knowledge Management Environment." Gaines, B. R. and M. Musen, eds. *Proceeding of the 11th Banff Knowledge Acquisition Workshop.* 1998.

Mayer, Richard J. et al. *Design Knowledge Management System (DKMS) Beta Test Report.* Ohio: Wright Patterson Air Force Base, Armstrong Laboratory, Air Force Material Command, 1993.

McKenna, B. et al., eds. *Online Information 98. Proceedings.* Oxford: Learned Information Europe Ltd, 1998.

Menou, Michel J. *Studies of the Impact of Electronic Networking on Development: Report of the Mid-Project Meeting of the CABECA Survey of African Internet Use.* Addis Ababa: Pan African Development Information System, 1998.

Milne, R. et al., eds. *Applications and Innovations in Expert Systems VI. Proceedings of ES98, the Eighteenth Annual International Conference of the British Computer Society Specialist Group on Expert Systems.* London: Springer-Verlag London Ltd, 1999.

Nixon, Carol et al., comps. *Internet Librarian '98: Proceedings of the Internet Librarian Conference.* Medford, NJ: Information Today, Inc., 1998.

Plaza, Enric, ed. *Knowledge Acquisition, Modelling and Management: 10th European Workshop, Ekaw '97, Sant Feliu De Guixols, Catalonia, Spain, 15-18 October 1997: Proceedings.* Berlin: Springer-Verlag, 1997.

"Proceedings of the First Knowledge & Information Management Conference (KIM'99)." *Information Services & Use* 19.01.

Prusak, Larry. "Managing Principal, IBM Global Services, Consulting Group." Presentation at the Conference Board Conference. The 1998 Conference of Knowledge Management and Organizational Learning in Chicago, IL. (16 April 1998).

Puppe, F., ed. *XPS-99: Knowledge-Based Systems. Survey and Future Directions. 5th Biannual German Conference Proceedings.* Berlin: Springer-Verlag, 1999.

Raimond, Paul. "From the Conference Scene." *European Management Journal* 16.02 (April 1998): 242-245.

Raitt, David Z. et al. *Online Information 97 Proceedings: 21st International Online Information Meeting.* Oxford: Learned Information Europe Ltd., 1997.

Raitt, David Z. et al. *Online Information 98: Proceedings.* Oxford: Learned Information Europe Ltd, 1998.

Reardon, Denis F. "Knowledge Management: The Discipline for Information and Science Professionals." Paper submitted to the 64th IFLA General Conference in Amsterdam. (16-21 August 1998).

Remeikis, L. A. and E. Koska. "Organization for Knowledge: Developing a Knowledge Management System." William, Martha E., ed. *Proceedings of the 17th National Online Meeting.* Medford, NJ: Information Today, Inc., 1996.

Roushan, G. and M. Bobeva. "The Potential of Intranets as a Tool for Knowledge Management: The New Challenge for IS Professionals." Brooks, L. and C. Kimble, eds. *Proceedings of the 4th UKAIS Conference.* Maidenhead, UK: McGraw-Hill Publishing Co., 1999.

"SAE '99 International Congress & Exposition." *Design News* 54.04 (15 February 1999): 93.

Sanderson, S. M. "New Approaches to Strategy: New Ways of Thinking for the Millennium." *Management Decision Conference 36, No. 01. Managing in the New Millennium Conference, 12-14 June 1997.* United Kingdom: MCB University Press, 1998.

Santos, J. et al. "VERITAS-An Application for Knowledge Verification." *Proceedings of the 11th International Conference on Tools with Artificial Intelligence.* Los Alamitos, CA: IEEE Computer Society, 1999.

"Seeking the There There." *Intelligent Enterprise* 02.01 (05 January 1999): 01.

Senge, Peter. "Organizational Learning." Paper presented at the 16th Annual International Conferences of the Strategic Management Society in Phoenix, AZ. (November, 1996).

Simoudis, E. et al. "Knowledge Acquisition in Case-Based Reasoning: ...and Then a Miracle Happens." *Proceedings of the 1992 Florida AI Research Symposium*. 1992.

Skyrme, D. J. "From Information to Knowledge Management: Are You Prepared?" Raitt, David Z. et al., eds. *Online Information 97 Proceedings: 21st International Online Information Meeting.* Oxford: Learned Information Europe Ltd, 1997.

Soe, L. L. and M. Roldan. "Ecommerce Technologies: Managing the Bleeding Edge." *Proceedings of the Americas Conference on Information Systems* (1998): 348-350.

Swartz, L. H. "Implicit Knowledge (Tacit Knowing), Connoisseurship, and the Common Law Tradition." Paper presented at the faculty workshop of the University at Buffalo School of Law in Buffalo, NY. (11 April 1997).

Taylor, Volney. "Technology Innovation and Processing Information: Content and Context." *Vital Speeches of the Day* 65.07: 201-204.

Thalheim, B. et al. *MFDBS 91: 3rd Symposium on Mathematical Fundamentals of Database and Knowledge Based Systems, Rostock, Germany, 06-09 May 1991: Proceedings.* Berlin: Springer-Verlag, 1991.

Weiss, Andrew and Georgiy Nikitin. "Performance of Czech Companies by Ownership Structure." Paper presented at the William Davidson Institute at the University of Michigan Conference on Finance in Transition Economies. (May 1998).

Zytkow, Jan M. and Mohamed Quafafou. *Principles of Data Mining and Knowledge Discovery: Second European Symposium, Pkdd '98, Nantes, France, September 1998: Proceedings.* Berlin: Springer-Verlag, 1998.

KNOWLEDGE MANAGEMENT AND COMPETITIVE INTELLIGENCE

The acquisition of knowledge is the core function of Knowledge Management. Does it matter how this information is acquired? Absolutely. When one thinks of Competitive Intelligence, it has conjured up visions of Industrial Espionage replete with trench coats, fedoras, and whispered conversations in alleys. That, of course, is one of the more unsavory ways of compiling Competitive Intelligence. Is that the only way? Of course not.

The ability to ethically acquire the Competitive Intelligence a firm needs to compete is a skill that has been not given its just due. In order to get quality information, an employee must be a skilled researcher, willing to share knowledge (sources), and be willing to look to others for assistance as needed. Competitive Intelligence is one of the concrete ways in which the people, processes, and technology of a Knowledge Management program can show the financial benefits of adopting this strategy.

The organization with the best Competitive Intelligence division will have a substantial advantage in the workplace whether it involves anticipating market changes, knowing what one's customer needs, or updating production practices. There is no area of business in which Competitive Intelligence cannot play a proactive role. As any organizational manager knows, the firm that is the most proactive in its business undertakings is the one that will succeed. Competitive Intelligence, if used correctly and in a timely manner can be a great contributor to the success of an organization. If the available Competitive Intelligence is not used, then the firm will soon be in dire straits.

As the reader looks through this Bibliography, the word, "competitive" is used often in the titles of articles, books, and journals. Competition is a fact of life. Any legitimate advantage that can be taken by an organization can only allow it a greater chance for success.

There are many legitimate ways to collect data, and it is truly a skill to do it well. This group of articles discusses some of the legitimate ways in which this truly necessary component of Knowledge Management can be done in an ethical manner.

Abramson, Gary. "All Along the Watchtower." *CIO* 12.19 (15 July 1999): S24-S30.

Andrewartha, Letitia. "Using Business Intelligence to Achieve a Sustainable Competitive Advantage." *Tidskrift for Dokumentation* 54.04 (1999): 103-110.

Anthes, Gary H. "Competitive Intelligence." *Computerworld* 32.27 (06 July 1998): 62.

Auditore, Peter J. "BI/DW in the Millennium." *Enterprise Systems Journal* 15.01 (January 2000): 20.

Avila, Larry. "Researchers Target 'Secret' Corporate Information." *Business Ledger* 08.09 (01 May 2000): 01, 18.

Bergsman, Steve. "Corporate Spying Goes Mainstream." *CFO: The Magazine for Senior Financial Executives* 13.12 (December 1994): 24.

Bolita, Dan. "Building a Business Intelligence System Requires Intelligent Building Blocks." *KMWorld* 08.05 (May 1999): 26-27.

Boucher, J. "Sneak a Peek at the Competition." *Bank Marketing* 28.03: 32-35.

"Bridging the Data Divide—Competitive Intelligence Is Becoming an Essential Tool to Keep Ahead of the Pack." *European Chemical News* (1999): 27.

Campanelli, Melissa. "I Spy." *Entrepreneur* 27.06 (June 1999): 48.

"Cipher Delivers Powerful Knowledge Management and Competitive Intelligence Products Based on IBM Middleware." *Business Wire* 1535 (08 June 1999).

"CISource." *Online* 22.04 (July-August 1998): 10.

Cohen, Andy. "The Misuse of Competitive Intelligence." *Sales & Marketing Management* 150.03 (March 1998): 13.

"Competitive Intelligence Guide." *Information Today* 13.08 (September 1996): 01-02.

"Competitive Intelligence Leader Predicts Service Convergence Between Commerce and Networks." *Business Wire* 1261 (13 October 1998).

"Competitive Intelligence Professionals Mark 10th Anniversary of Their Society." *Information Today* 13.05 (May 1996): 17-19.

Crimmins, Francis et al. "TetraFusuin: Information Discovery on the Internet." *IEEE Intelligent Systems* 14.04 (July-August 1999): 55-62.

"Current Analysis Extends Competitive Intelligence to Third-Party Channel to Drive Additional Sales." *Business Wire* (21 September 1998).

Dover, Gary. "Knowledge Warriors: Intelligence Specialists in the 21st Century." *Competitive Intelligence Magazine* 02.01 (January-March 1999): 29-33.

"Economic Espionage Explosion." *Security* 35.05 (May 1998): 14-19.

"Face-to-Face: Staples CEO Tom Stemberg on Competitive Intelligence." *Inc.* 18.12 (August 1998): 45.

Fine, N. "Competitive Intelligence: An External Threat and an Internal Requirement." *Computer Security Journal* 11.02 (Fall 1995): 75-78.

Freeman, Olivia. "Competitor Intelligence: Information or Intelligence?" *Business Information Review* 16.02 (June 1999): 71-77.

Gibbons, P. T. and J. E. Prescott. "Parallel Competitive Intelligence Processes in Organisations." *International Journal of Technology Management* 11.01-02 (1996): 162-178.

Gieskes, Hans. "Competitive Intelligence at LEXIS-NEXIS." *Competitive Intelligence Review* 11.02 (Second Quarter 2000): 04-11.

Green, William. "I Spy." *Forbes* 161.08 (20 April 1998): 90-94.

Hart, G.-M. "Knowledge Management and Competitive Intelligence in Australia." *Journal of AGSI* 07.02 (Fall 1998): 36-40.

Johnson, Arik. "CI Helps Build Stake in Future." *KMWorld* 08.07 (July 1999): 20.

Johnson, Arik. "Competitive Intelligence Workflow: From *ad hoc* Research to Environmental Scanning." *KMWorld* 08.10 (October 1999): 18-19.

Johnson, Arik. "E-businesses without CI Are Like Ships Without Radar Lost in Fog." *KMWorld* 09.01 (2000): 28-30.

Kahaner, Larry. "Seven Ways to Get the Skinny on a Company." *Executive Female* 19.04 (July-August 1996): 21-23.

Kassler, Helene S. "Competitive Intelligence on the Web." *EContent* 22.04 (August-September 1999): 15.

Kassler, Helene S. "Mining the Internet for Competitive Intelligence: How to Track and Sift for Golden Nuggets." *Online* 21.05 (September-October 1997): 34-38, 40-42, 45.

Kennedy, Shirley Duglin. "Competitive Intelligence on the Web 101." *Information Today* (01 October 1998): 40.

Klein, Mark. "Tech Is Key to a Knowledge-Based Game." *National Underwriter* 103.40 (04 October 1999): 18-20.

Lamont, Judith. "CI Tools Enable More Confident Business Decisions." *KMWorld* 08.07 (July 1999): 21, 29.

Levitas, E. et al. "Competitive Intelligence and Tacit Knowledge Development in Strategic Alliances." *Competitive Intelligence Review* 08.02 (1997): 392-398.

Lorge, Sarah. "Why It Pays to be Curious." *Sales & Marketing Management* 150.08 (August 1998): 76.

Malhotra, Yogesh. "Competitive Intelligence Programs: An Overview." http://www. brint.com/papers/ciover.htm

McBride, Hugh. "They Snoop to Conquer." *Canadian Business* 70.08 (July 1997): 45-47.

Miller, Jerry P. "Some Competitive Intelligence Advice." *Information Today* 16.07 (July-August 1999): 56.

Moon, Mary Gemmel. "Effective Use of Information & Competitive Intelligence." *Information Outlook* 04.02 (February 2000): 17-20.

"Not a Smart Move." *Industry Week* 247.04 (16 February 1998): 16.

Ojala, Marydee and Jesper Vissing Laursen. "HEAD to HEAD for Competitive Intelligence." *Online* 22.06 (November 1998): 62.

Pagell, R. "Economic Espionage and Strategic Intelligence." *Journal of AGSI* 08.01 (March 1999): 36-43.

Pirttila, Anneli. "Competitor Information and Competitive Knowledge Management in a Large, Industrial Organization (NETWORKS)." *Dissertation Abstracts International* 59.02: 265-439.

Powell, Tim. "Tech Knowledge: Disinformation about Knowledge Management." *Competitive Intelligence Magazine* 03.01 (January-March 2000): 51-52.

Robinson, Edward A. "China's Spies Target Corporate America." *Fortune* 137.06 (30 March 1998): 118-121.

Rodenberg, J. H. A. M. "The Five Phases Model of Implementing Competitive Intelligence in the Organisation." *Journal of AGSI* 08.03 (November 1999): 80-83.

Shaker, Steven M. and Mark P. Gembicki. "Competitive Intelligence: A Futurist's Perspective." *Competitive Intelligence Magazine* 02.01 (January-March 1999): 24-27.

Shelfer, Katherine. "The Intersection of Knowledge Management and Competitive Intelligence: Smartcards and Electronic Commerce." Srikantaiah, Kanti and Michael E. D. Koenig, eds. *Knowledge Management for the Information Professional.* Medford, NJ: Information Today, 1999.

Short, Thomas. "Components of a Knowledge Strategy: Keys to Successful Knowledge Management." Srikantaiah, Kanti and Michael E. D. Koenig, eds. *Knowledge Management for the Information Professional.* Medford, NJ: Information Today, 1999.

Simon, Neil J. "CI Personnel: Requirements for the Multicultural Organization." *Competitive Intelligence Magazine* 02.01 (January-March 1999): 43-44.

Simon, Neil J. "The Effects of Organizational Culture on the CI Process." *Competitive Intelligence Review* 10.01 (First Quarter 1999): 62-70.

"Special Issue: Competitive Intelligence." *Library Trends* 43.02 (Fall 1994).

Teo, Thompson S. H. "Using the Internet for Competitive Intelligence in Singapore." *Competitive Intelligence Review* 11.02 (Second Quarter 2000): 61-70.

Teresko, John. "Information Rich, Knowledge Poor? Data Warehouses Transform Information into Competitive Intelligence." *Industry Week* 248.03 (01 February 1999): 19-20.

Vedder, R. G. and M. T. Vanecek. "Competitive Intelligence for IT Resource Planning: Some Lessons Learned." *Information Strategy: The Executive's Journal* 15.01 (Fall 1998): 29-36.

Vedder, Richard G. et al. "CEO and CIO Perspectives on Competitive Intelligence." *Communications of the ACM* 42.08 (August 1999): 108.

Vella, Carolyn M. and John J. McGonagle. "Profiling in Competitive Analysis." *Competitive Intelligence Review* 11.02 (Second Quarter 2000): 20-30.

Wimmer, Bruce. "A Spy in the Boardroom." *Asian Business* 35.03 (March 1999): 54-55.

WEB SITES

I am a big fan of print in any format—books, journals, newspapers, etc. The Electronic Age of the last several years has been making significant changes in our daily lives. Much of the information that was only available in print is now available electronically: books, journals, newspapers, etc. In order to remain competitive, an organization must be active in both arenas—electronic and print.

Among the many technological advances that have come in the recent past, the Internet and its many and varied uses may be the single most influential way of communicating since the telephone. Easily accessible, fast, and relatively inexpensive, the Internet and its accompanying technology can carry text, pictures, video, and even voice transmission in a fraction of the time it used to take to communicate with others. The greatest benefit of electronic communication is speed. Once this book was printed, it becomes a static artifact. If I find a journal article on eCommerce, it must wait until the next edition of this book is printed. It can be posted electronically as soon as it is located.

About five years ago, about 20 percent of the Fortune 500 companies had Web sites. Now, the figure is 100 percent. Just having and maintaining a Web site is not enough. It must be accessible (easily located), authoritative, current, professionally maintained, and user-friendly in order to be effective. The greatest benefit of these properties is currency. As stated above, as events occur, they can be posted to the Web site and made available to both customers and users.

As new technology comes into use, decisions must be made to determine the value (if any) of the new technology to the organization. Just because something is new doesn't mean that every organization should use it. Care should be exercised to ensure that the Web site user is not overwhelmed by graphics and other paraphernalia that detract from the value of the site.

The Web sites that follow are just a few among the many that exist. The Web sites are not indexed, just listed here in alphabetical order. All were viewed between January 2000 and July 2000.

13 Update
http://www.skyrme.com

AIAI (Artificial Intelligence)
http://www.aiai.ed.ac.uk

American Productvity and Quality Center
http://www.apqc.org

Argentine Society for Informatics and Operations Research (SADIO)
http://www.uba.ar/wwws/sadio/homepage-ingles.html

Arthur Andersen
http://www.arthurandersen.com

Artificial Intelligence Applications Institute Knowledge Management Links
http://www.aiai.ed.ac.uk/~alm/kamlnks.html

Association for Computing Machinery Knowledge Management General
Information and Resources
http://www.acm.org/siggroup/knowledge.html

Aurora WDC
http://www.aurorawdc.com/index.htm

Australian Human Resources Institute
http://ahri.com.au

Awaken Technology
http://www.awaken.com

Binder Riha Associates
http://www.binder-riha.com/publications.htm

Booz, Allen & Hamilton
http://www.bah.com/greatideas/index.html

Brint: Knowledge Management and Organizational Learning
http://www.brint.com

British Council Information Exchange
http://www.britishcouncil.org/infoexch/index.htm

British Telecommunications Reading List
http://www.bt.com/innovation/exhibition/knowledge_management/
furtherreading.htm

Buckman Laboratories
http://www.knowledge-nurture.com

Business Process Resource Centre
http://bprc.warwick.ac.uk

A Business Researcher's Interests
http://www.brint.com/interest.html

CAB International (CABI)
http://www.cabi.org

Cambridge Technology Partners
http://www.ctp.com/wwt/know/index.html

Canadian Institute of Competitive Intelligence
www.cici-icic.ca

Center for Global Studies (CGS), Houston Advanced Research Center
(HARC)
http://www.harc.edu

Center for Knowledge Management at Dominican University,
River Forest, IL
http://www.dom.edu/Academic/GSLIS/KMInfo.html

Centre for Landscape Research Internetwork (University of Toronto)
http://www.clr.utoronto.ca:1080

Centre for Policy Research on Science and Technology/Management of
Technology (CPROST/MOT)
http://mot.cprost.sfu.ca

CIO Magazine Online
http://www.cio.com

cio.com Knowledge Management Resource Center
http://www.cio.com/forums/knowledge/

Cognitive Engineering and Decision Making Technical Group (CEDM-TG)
http://www.ie.msstate.edu

Cogos Consulting, Inc.
http://www.cogos.com/cogosweb/cogoswebsite.nsf/?Open

Collaborative Strategies
http://www.collaborate.com

Columbia Institute for Tele-Information (CITI)
http://www.ctr.Columbia.edu

Commercenet
http://www.commercenet.com

Commonwealth of Learning Information Resource Centre
http://www.col.org/irc/irc.htm

Community KM Glossary
http://knowledgecreators.com/km/kes/glossary.htm

Competencies for Special Librarians of the 21st Century
http://www.sla.org/professional/comp.html

Competia.com (Competitive Intelligence)
http://www.competia.com/

Computer Security Laboratory, University of California at Davis
http://seclab.cs.ucdavis.edu

Consulting and Audit Canada
http://w3.pwgsc.gc.ca

CoreLAN Communications, Inc.
http://www.corelan.com

Database of Best Practices on Indigenous Knowledge
http://www.unesco.org/most/bpindi.htm

Dataware Technologies, Inc.
http://www.dataware.dk/uindex.htm

Delphi Group
http://www.delphigroup.com

Delphi Resource Center (Technology)
http://www.webcom.com/~optimax/delphi/delphi.html

Delphic Interactive
http://www.delphic.co.uk/

Department of Knowledge Systems at the Institute of Scientific and
Industrial Research, Osaka University
http://www.ei.sanken.osaka-u.ac.jp

Digital Commerce Center
http://www.ec2.edu/dccenter/index.html

Digital Systems Research Center
http://www.research.digital.com

Distributed Systems Technology Centre
http://www.dstc.edu.au

Document Management/Knowledge Management Internet Directory
http://www.dm-kmdirectory.com/

Ecommerce Resources
http://www.commerce.net/resources/

Economic Intelligence and Commercial Intelligence on the Web
http://www.fas.org/irp/wwwecon.html

Ernst & Young
http://www.ey.com

Ernst & Young Center for Business Innovation
http://www.businessinnovation.ey.com

Federation for Enterprise Knowledge Development
http://www.fend.es

FID Knowledge Forum
http://fid.conicyt.cl:8000

Financial Management Association International
http://www.fma.org

Forbes ASAP
http://www.forbes.com

Fortuity Consulting
http://www.fortuity.com

Fulcrum Technologies Inc.
http://www.pcdocs.com

Gartner Group
http://gartner6.gartnerweb.com/public/static/home/home.html

Graduate School of Business, University of Texas at Austin
http://www.bus.utexas.edu/kman

grapeVine Technologies
http://www.gvt.com

Group Decision Support Systems
http://www.gdss.com

Harvard Institute for International Development (HIID)
http://www.hiid.harvard.edu

Hci
http://www.hci.com.au/hcisite/

Healthcare Knowledge Management (HKM) Consortium
http://www.healthkm.com/aboutmkm.htm

Hyperknowledge
http://www.hyperknowledge.com

Ibex Knowledge Systems Knowledge Management Links
http://www.ibex.ch/links/

IBM Knowledge Management
http://www-4.ibm.com/software/data/knowledge/

IBM Think Leadership
http://www.ibm.com/thinkmag

Idea Exchange
http://www.sol-ne.org

Information World Review
http://www.iwr.co.uk/iwr/

Institute for Informatics in Design and Production (IIEF) in Berlin GmbH.
(in German)
http://www.iief.de

Institute for Learning Technologies, Columbia University
http://www.ilt.columbia.edu

Institute for Operations Research and the Management Sciences
(INFORMS)
http://www.informs.org

Institute for Technology and Enterprise
http://www.ite.poly.edu/htmls/index.html

Institute for Telecooperation Technology (TKT)
http://www.darmstadt.gmd.de

Institute of Electrical and Electronics Engineers, Inc.
http://www.ieee.org

Intelligent Enterprise
http://www.intelligententerprise.com/

International Knowledge Management Newsletter
http://www.mjm.co.uk/knowledge/repch1.html

Integral Performance Group
http://knowledgecreators.com

Integrated Reasoning Group
http://ai.iit.nrc.ca/IR_public/english.html

Intellectual Capital Home Page/Dr. Nick Bontis, Director of the Institute
for Intellectual Capital Research
http://www.business.mcmaster.ca/mktg/nbontis/ic

Intelligence Online
http://www.indigo-net.com

International Institute for Management Development
http://www.imd.ch/

International Journal of Information Management Table of Contents
http://www.elsevier.com/inca/publications/store/3/0/4/3/4/

International Knowledge Management Newsletter
http://www.mjm.co.uk/knowledge/repch1.html

Interoperable Systems Research Centre
http://www.soi.city.ac.uk

Intramark
http://www.intramark.com/resources/

Intranet Design Magazine
http://idm.internet.com/

Intranet Research Center
http://www.cio.com

ISWorld Net
http://www.isworld.org

Kaieteur Institute for Knowledge Management
http://www.kikm.org/services.html

Keane, Inc.
http://www.keane.com/services/index.html

Kentucky Initiative for Knowledge Management at the University of Kentucky
http://gatton.gws.uky.edu/dsis/ky_init.htm

KMC International
http://www.km.org/

KMCentral.com
http://www.kmcentral.com/

KMetaSite
http://www.kmetasite.org/

KMTool—A Knowledge Management Resource
http://www.kmtool.net

KMWorld Magazine
http://kmonline.com
http://www.kmworld.com/

Knowledge Ability
http://www.knowab.co.uk/km

Knowledge Associates
http://www.knowledgeassociates.com/

Knowledge Associates International
http://www.knowledgeassociates.com

Knowledge Discovery Associates
http://www.knowledge-discovery.com

Knowledge Garden
http://www.co-i-l.com

Knowledge Inc.
http://www.knowledgeinc.com

Knowledge Magazine
http://www.mediaaccess.com

Knowledge Management
http://www.mbs.umd.edu/is/malavi/icis-97-KMS/index.htm

Knowledge Management
http://www.vknowledge.net/

Knowledge Management Benchmarking Association
www.kmba.org

Knowledge Management Consortium
http://www.km.org

Knowledge Management Consultants
http://www.kmc.co.za

Knowledge Management Discussion
http://www.alvea.com/wwwboard/wwwboard.html

The Knowledge Management Forum
http://www.km-forum.org

Knowledge Management Group at Charles Stuart University in Australia
http://www.csu.edu.au

Knowledge Management Links
http://www.computerworld.com/home/features.nsf/All/980608kmlinks

Knowledge Management Magazine
http://www.knowledge-management.co.uk/kbase/index.asp

Knowledge Management Network
http://kmn.cibit.nl/index.html

Knowledge Management News
http://www.kmnews.com

Knowledge Management Reference Sites
http://cis.kaist.ac.kr/research/kmsite.htm

Knowledge Management Research Center
http://www.kmresource.com/

Knowledge Management Resource Center
http://www.cio.com/forums/knowledge/resource_links.html

Knowledge Management Resources
http://www.skyrme.com/resource/kmres.htm

Knowledge Management Resources
http://www.smithweaversmith.com/resource.htm

Knowledge Management Resources at Information and Library Science at
the University of North Carolina
http://ils.unc.edu/~kellj/path/conf.htm

Knowledge Management Resources, Knowledge Management Information,
Knowledge Management Links
http://ftp.jump.net/~curt/meredith/knowledgemanagement.html

Knowledge Management Think Tank ™
http://www.brint.com/wwwboard/wwwboard.html

Knowledge Management, Workflow & Organization Learning
http://www.insead.fr/CALT/

Knowledge Management World
http://www.kmworld.com

Knowledge Media Institute
http://kmi.open.ac.uk

Knowledge Praxis
http://www.mediaaccess.com

Knowledge Research Institute
http://www.knowledgeresearch.com

Knowledge Systems & Research, Inc.
http://www.ksrinc.com/

Knowledge Technology Centre
http://www.psychology.nottingham.ac.uk/research/ktc/

Knowledge Transfer International/KM Metazine
http://www.ktic.com

Knowledgeshop
http://www.knowledgeshop.com/

Knowledgies
http://www.knowledgies.com

Learned Information Europe, Ltd.
http://www.learned.co.uk
http://www.oxfordshire.co.uk/data/015041.html

Learning Organizations Home Page
http://www.albany.edu/~kl7686/learnorg.html

Legenda
http://www.legenda.com/

Library Research Service
http://www.lrs.org

Management and Technology Dictionary
http://www.euro.net/innovation/Management_Base/Mantec.Dictionary.html

Management Science: Knowledge Management
http://www.bpubs.com/Management_Science/Knowledge_Management/

McDowell Consulting
http://www.mcdowellconsult.net/mcnet.nsf/?Open

Mercer Management
http://www.mercermc.com

Metacode
http://www.metacode.com/flashindex.html

Microsoft Corporation Knowledge Management and Collaboration
Training Roadmap
http://www.microsoft.com/TechNet/exchange/collabrm.asp

MIT Society for Organizational Learning
http://learning.mit.edu

Modus Operandi
http://www.modusoperandi.com

The Montague Institute Review
http://www.montague.com

National Institute for Working Life
http://www.niwl.se/default_en.asp

New Directions for Policy
http://www.ndpolicy.com

Open Directory—Reference: Knowledge Management
http://dmoz.org/Reference/Knowledge_Management/

Outsights—Knowledge Management
http://www.outsights.com/systems/kmgmt/kmgmt.htm

Paradigm Shift International
http://www.parshift.com

PriceWaterhouseCoopers
http://www.pwcglobal.com

Research Institute for Knowledge Systems
http://www.riks.nl

Romer, Paul Home Page
http://www.stanford.edu/~promer

ServiceWare.com
http://www.knowledgebridge.com

Skandia—Intellectual Capital
http://www2.skandia.com/skandia/idx_sitemap.htm

Society of Competitive Intelligence Professionals
http://www.scip.org

Special Libraries Association Knowledge Management Page
http://www.sla.org/membership/irc/knowledg.html

Special Libraries Association, Toronto, Canada
http://www.sla.org/chapter/ctor/toolbox/km/kmfrm.htm

Special Libraries Association's Competitive Intelligence Links
http://www.sla.org/membership/irc/intell.html

Stanford Knowledge Systems Laboratory
http://ksl.stanford.edu

Sveiby Knowledge Management
http://www.sveiby.com.au

Tacit Knowledge Management
http://www.tacitkm.com/

The Technology Broker
http://www.tbroker.co.uk

Teleos
http://www.knowledgebusiness.com/top.html

Teltech
http://www.teltech.com

TFPL, Ltd.
http://www.tfpl.com

Topic Area: Knowledge Management/ Intellectual Capital
http://bookwatch.com.au/BB/Topic/Knowledge.bbd

UCSF Center for Knowledge Management
http://www.ckm.ucsf.edu

United States Government Electronic Commerce Policy
http://www.ecommerce.gov/

University of Amsterdam Knowledge Management Archive
ftp://swi.psy.uva.nl/pub/knowman/

University of Colorado at Denver, School of Education: Organizational
Learning and Knowledge Management
http://carbon.cudenver.edu/~mryder/itc_data/org_learning.html

University of Sydney, Technology Introduction to Knowledge Management
http://www.uts.edu.au/fac/hss/Departments/DIS/km/introduct.htm

University of Texas Knowledge Management Server
http://www.bus.utexas.edu/kman

VerticalNet E-commerce
http://www.verticalnet.com

Virtual Library on Knowledge Management
http://www.brint.com/km

Work Space International's Information and
Knowledge Management Resources
http://www.workspaceinternational.com/workspacelinks.htm

Working by Wire
http://www.knowab.co.uk/ka.html

Working By Wire White Paper: Team Knowledge Management:
A Computer-Mediated Approach
http://www.knowab.co.uk/wbwteam.html

World Bank Group Knowledge Sharing
http://www.worldbank.org/ks/

World Resources Institute
www.wri.org

WWW Resources on Knowledge Management
http://www-personal.umich.edu/~wfan/km.htm

Xerox Corporation
http://www.xerox.com/go/xrx/knowledgest/Knowledge.jsp

Yankee Group
www.yankeegroup.com

Yogesh Malhotra's Knowledge Management Artefacts
http://www.brint.com/knowledge.htm

VIDEOS

The videos listed here are not grouped into subheadings. This list contains those videos produced with "Intellectual Capital" or "Knowledge Management" as their primary focus as taken from the inventories of amazon.com and barnesandnoble.com. These two sources were selected because of the sheer volume of their respective inventories, and the videos should be among the most current available.

These videos will be very helpful as an adjunct to a lecture, seminar, a training session, or for use by the Auditory Learner.

Data Mining for Business Professionals. Syosset, NY: Computer Channel Inc., 1997.

Getting Out of the Box: The Knowledge Management Opportunity. Special Libraries Association, 1996.

Intelligent Agents. Syosset, NY: Computer Channel Inc., 1997.

Knowledge Management. Manchester: EBC, 2000.

Knowledge Management Company. Special Libraries Association, 1997.

Into the Future: On the Preservation of Knowledge in the Electronic Age. Produced and Directed by Terry Sanders. American Film Foundation, 1997.

APPENDIX: DATABASE LIST

Access to sources provided by the Center for Knowledge Management at Dominican University, River Forest, IL.

ABI INFORM

Article First

Books in Print

British Education Index

Contents First

Delphes Eurpoean Business

ECO

EIU: The Economist Intelligence Unit

ERIC

Fortune Magazine

Harvard Business Review

IAC
   Industry Express
   Management Contents

Newsearch

Trade & Industry Database

Information Science Abstracts

INFOTRAC

Expanded Academic ASAP

Business and Company ASAP

INSPEC

Library and Information Science Abstracts

National Technical Information Service

NetFirst

PAIS International

Papers First

Periodical Abstracts

Proceedings

Wilson Business Abstracts

Wilson Humanities Abstracts

Wilson Library Literature

Wilson Select

Wilson Social Sciences Abstracts

WorldCat

AUTHOR INDEX

More Books from Information Today, Inc.

The Web of Knowledge:
A Festschrift in Honor of Eugene Garfield

Edited by Blaise Cronin
and Helen Barsky Atkins

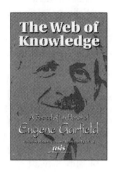

Dr. Eugene Garfield, the founder of the Institute for Scientific Information (ISI), has devoted his life to the creation and development of the multidisciplinary *Science Citation Index*. The index, a unique resource for scientists, scholars, and researchers in virtually every field of intellectual endeavor, has been the foundation for a multidisciplinary research community. This new ASIST monograph is the first to comprehensively address the history, theory, and practical applications of the *Science Citation Index* and to examine its impact on scholarly and scientific research 40 years after its inception. In bringing together the analyses, insights, and reflections of more than 35 leading lights, editors Cronin and Atkins have produced both a comprehensive survey of citation indexing and analysis and a beautifully realized tribute to Eugene Garfield and his vision.

hardbound • ISBN 1-57387-099-4

ASIST Members $39.60   Non-Members $49.50

Introductory Concepts in Information Science

Melanie J. Norton

Melanie J. Norton presents a unique introduction to the practical and theoretical concepts of information science while examining the impact of the Information Age on society. Drawing on recent research into the field, as well as from scholarly and trade publications, the monograph provides a brief history of information science and coverage of key topics, including communications and cognition, information retrieval, bibliometrics, modeling, economics, information policies, and the impact of information technology on modern management. This is an essential volume for graduate students, practitioners, and any professional who needs a solid grounding in the field of information science.

hardbound • ISBN 1-57387-087-0

ASIST Members $31.60   Non-Members $39.50

Knowledge Management for the Information Professional

Edited by T. Kanti Srikantaiah
and Michael Koenig

Written from the perspective of the information community, this book examines the business community's recent enthusiasm for "Knowledge Management." With contributions from 26 leading KM practitioners, academicians, and information professionals, editors Srikantaiah and Koenig bridge the gap between two distinct perspectives, equipping information professionals with the tools to make a broader and more effective contribution in developing KM systems and creating a knowledge management culture within their organizations.

hardbound • ISBN 1-57387-079-X

ASIST Members $35.60   Non-Members $44.50

ARIST 33
Annual Review of Information Science and Technology

Edited by Martha E. Williams

Since 1966, ARIST has been continuously at the cutting edge in contributing a useful and comprehensive view of the broad field of information science and technology. ARIST reviews numerous topics within the field and ultimately provides this annual source of ideas, trends, and references to the literature. A master plan for the series encompasses the entire field in all its aspects, and topics for the annual volume are selected on the basis of timeliness and an assessment of reader interest. The newest edition of ARIST covers topics that fit within the fundamental structure as follows: Planning Information Systems and Services, Basic Techniques and Technologies, and Applications.

hardbound • ISBN 1-57387-065-X

ASIST Members $79.95   **Non-Members $99.95**

Information Management for the Intelligent Organization, Second Edition

Chun Wei Choo

The intelligent organization is one that is skilled at marshalling its information resources and capabilities, transforming information into knowledge, and using this knowledge to sustain and enhance its performance in a restless environment. The objective of this newly updated and expanded book is to develop an understanding of how an organization may manage its information processes more effectively in order to achieve these goals. This book is a must read for senior managers and administrators, information managers, information specialists and practitioners, information technologists, and anyone whose work in an organization involves acquiring, creating, organizing, or using knowledge.

hardbound • ISBN 1-57387-057-9

ASIST Members $31.60   **Non-Members $39.50**

Millennium Intelligence
Understanding & Conducting Competitive Intelligence in the Digital Age

Edited by Jerry Miller

With contributions from the world's leading business intelligence practitioners, here is a tremendously informative and practical look at the CI process, how it is changing, and how it can be managed effectively in the Digital Age. Loaded with case studies, tips, and techniques, chapters include What Is Intelligence?; The Skills Needed to Execute Intelligence Effectively; Information Sources Used for Intelligence; The Legal and Ethical Aspects of Intelligence; Corporate Security and Intelligence ...and much more!

softbound • ISBN 0-910965-28-5

$29.95

Internet Business Intelligence
How to Build a Big Company System on a Small Company Budget
David Vine

According to author David Vine, business success in the competitive, global marketplace of the 21st century will depend on a firm's ability to use information effectively—and the most successful firms will be those that harness the Internet to create and maintain a powerful information edge. In *Internet Business Intelligence*, Vine explains how any company—large or small—can build a complete, low-cost Internet-based business intelligence system that really works. If you're fed up with Internet hype and wondering "where's the beef?," you'll appreciate this savvy, no-nonsense approach to using the Internet to solve everyday business problems and to stay one step ahead of the competition.

softbound • ISBN 0-910965-35-8

$29.95

Super Searchers Do Business
The Online Secrets of Top Business Researchers
Mary Ellen Bates • Edited by Reva Basch

Super Searchers Do Business probes the minds of 11 leading researchers who use the Internet and online services to find critical business information. Through her in-depth interviews, Mary Ellen Bates—a business super searcher herself—gets the pros to reveal how they choose online sources, evaluate search results, and tackle the most challenging business research projects. Loaded with expert tips, techniques, and strategies, this is the first title in the exciting new "Super Searchers" series, edited by Reva Basch. If you do business research online, or plan to, let *Super Searchers Do Business* be your guide.

softbound • ISBN 0-910965-33-1

$24.95

The Extreme Searcher's Guide To Web Search Engines
A Handbook for the Serious Searcher
Randolph Hock

"Extreme searcher" Randolph (Ran) Hock—internationally respected Internet trainer and authority on Web search engines—offers advice designed to help you get immediate results. Ran not only shows you what's "under the hood" of the major search engines, but explains their relative strengths and weaknesses, reveals their many (and often overlooked) special features, and offers tips and techniques for searching the Web more efficiently and effectively than ever. Updates and links are provided at the author's Web site.

softbound • ISBN 0-910965-26-9 • $24.95
hardbound • ISBN 0-910965-38-2 • $34.95

For a publications catalog or to order, contact the publisher at
609-654-6266 or 800-300-9868 (EST), or log onto www.infotoday.com